IN
PURSUIT
OF ME

A Raw Journey of a Young Woman
Who Learned To Simultaneously
Pour and Stay Full

Lifting Up Downs Publications
Suffolk, Virginia
Have You Smiled From Your Soul Today?

In Pursuit Of Me
Copyright © 2014 by B. Dennis

Printed in the United States of America by CreateSpace
Lifting Up Downs Publications

www.bdennis.me

ISBN 978-0-692-31374-9

Cover Photo by Rashod Harris of The Rebel Society
Special Thanks to Eltonette Harris
Cover Design by Brandon Owens
Lifting Up Downs Logo by LaTesha Bourne
Edited by Dr. Angerina Jones

Lord God,
Your Kingdom Come,
Your Will be done,
On Earth,
As it is in Heaven.
I Love You.
Continue to compel me to make my actions say such.
In Jesus' Name,
Amen

DEDICATION

To Our Freedom
Transparency Leads to Deliverance

ACKNOWLEDGMENTS

To my very best friend, Jesus Christ: I am so elated that you call me friend. Thank you for walking with me and talking with me. To my Mommie: the wind beneath my wings, you elevated me to this point with your unwavering love, support, and reprove. You are the epitome of strength, perseverance, and agape love. To my favorite son in the whole wide world, GJ: you saved me. You are amazing no matter who tries to convince you that you are not. You are a game changer and a young man destined for greatness. I love you Bub. To my favorite daughter in the whole wide world, Gyasi: you confirmed that nothing is impossible. You are wonderful because that is what your name means. You show and will continue to show that you are wonderful. Thank you for your love and continuous affection. I love you Pretty Girl. To my Daddy, Everard Joshua Lord: thank you for loving me and always having a word of wisdom even if I do not want to hear it. I'm always listening. I love you. To Susan: thanks for always telling it like it is and being my Mommy Dearest. I love you. To Daddy Miles: thank you for teaching and giving me structure. I love you. To Uncle Paul: the first man to call me beautiful. I believed it because you treated me as such with your blunt and thorough direction. To my Titi, Vivian Smith: words cannot express my gratitude for your unconditional support. I cherish those morning phone calls telling me to get myself together and those naps on your couch. You truly have been my rock whether you know it or not. To my Granny: the strongest woman I know, you mean the world to me. When I do not feel strong, I think about you and automatically know I have strength because your blood is flowing through my veins. To Mami: thank you for your humor, strength, and love in Jesus. To Ma: I love you so much. To my get right and checking, my Auntie Tonya: thank you for always being "Just Tonya." I love you. To my Couster, Bria: the person that makes me laugh so hard I have to call you, my 2 am companion, also my checking and get right. You were and will always be my first best friend. You are wiser than your years. I love you so much. To Symone, my honey bunny, my free spirit: I am so proud of the young lady you are becoming. Pick your battles. Be set apart. Dare to be different. I love you. To Auntie Jenny: thank you for always keeping it real! I love you so much. To Tameka, my sissy: I love discovering how much we are alike. Thank you for always speaking what is on your mind. I love you. To Barry and Margie: thanks for accepting me as your own! Love y'all! To Ava and Gregory: Auntie loves you. To Renee: my Godmother, my Queen, my intercessor (yeah I know), I adore, love, and appreciate you. To Chelle, Bae: I appreciate you and I admire your grind. It is unmatched. God has used you so many times to be my voice of reason and peace. Words cannot express my love for you girl! I love you and my Jadey Wadey. To Jade: you are your greatest competition and you are destined for greatness. I love you beautiful. To Alisha and Nichole: thank you for being the siblings I never had and accepting me as your friend and sister, I love you both so much. To my brother, Mikey: you are wise beyond your years. Thank you for being set apart and living above the influence. To Caleb: Auntie loves you. To my cousin, London: thank you for not letting me be a prissy girly girl. Thank you for being an example of what a man is to your beautiful family! I love you all so much. To Sean: thank you for accepting me as your sister. I love you. Thank you to the Miles/McDaniel family for accepting me as your cousin, niece, and granddaughter. I love y'all. To my aunts, Sandy, Sharon, and Joi thank you for always being there for me and supporting me with your sweet spirits.

To my Auntie Aline: I miss you.

That moment when time stood still and I didn't care about the events for today and how I looked for them. That moment when time stood still and I didn't want to fulfill the promises I made to my kids just 10 minutes ago. That moment when time stood still and my heart ached for those who were closer to you than me. It stood still when I remembered your face. That smile and how you made me feel. Time stood still as I sat, closed my eyes, reminisced, and smiled warmly at your kindness and love. I was supposed to see you in June but due to time...

My chest tightened and I couldn't control the tears or my breath. That moment when time stood still to me, but really kept on going...

My kids always remind me that time keeps on going. My tears fell and GJ asked me for McDonald's because I still haven't cooked his big Saturday breakfast. And Gyasi just did a back flip from the backseat to the front seat.

That moment when time stood still but life reminded me that it keeps on going. Can't leave life unfinished. Can't leave dreams unfinished. You didn't.

GJ has to eat and Gyasi obviously needs to be tamed.

So I remember your smile and how your face would light up when I saw you. I remember your signature laugh that let me know you were somewhere near. I can feel your warm hugs and I cherish the cards that said Happy Birthday and how proud you were of me. Thank you for asking me if I was sure. Thank you for your kindness and your love Auntie A.

In moments when time stands still, I will envision you sitting close to God, admonishing me to keep going. I'll remember to make you both proud. I'll remember to be sure before I do anything. Everything about you and the way you made me feel reminds me to be kind and love others. You motivate me to keep on going when time stands still.

Therefore, since we are surrounded by such a huge crowd of witnesses to the life of faith, let us strip off every weight that slows us down, especially the sin that so easily trips us up. And let us run with endurance the race God has set before us (Hebrews 12:1).

To my Uncle Gregory: you are the epitome of an exceptional man. I love you. To my Aunt Trina: thank you for not allowing me to stay in my low place. Love you. To my Bertha Mae, Kenya: you mean the world to me. You are great! Never let your circumstances define your greatness! Keep pushing! I love you. To the Landers: I love you. To Mario: I love you. Thank you for being my friends. To my slew of family members to include uncles, aunts, and cousins on ALL SIDES of my family: I am grateful for your love and support. To The Girls: Crystal, big sis logist: you were there from the very beginning. Thank you for always being the authentic, intelligent, and humorous you. Jamika: you are one of a kind and you should be cherished, elevated, and admired. To Noelle: my little giant, my rock, my soul friend, you mean the WHOLE ENTIRE WORLD TO ME and that is all I could get out without becoming Sappy McSappington. To your parents, Robin and Landrum: thank you for being the example of tried and true love, I love and have always admired y'all. To LaTesha, my T-Beasting: I love you and you are strong beyond your strength. To Shyla Miles: this time next year. Keep pushing. I love you. To Elle: my accountability partner, the bold speaker, the administrator, the order bringer, the frog hater; thank you so much for your continued love and support. Thank you for not being afraid to tell me what thus saith the Lord. I love you. To Shod: thank you for also pushing me and holding me accountable. Without #ShodElle, this project would not have happened. To my push/pull partner, Ciara, thank you for loving me unconditionally and always being ready to intercede on my behalf, on the spot, real rap raw. I love you! To Chanel: thank you for believing in me! I love you girl! To Doctor Angerina: I admire you so much. Thank you for being a part of my foundation. Thank you for being a woman in whom I can emulate. Thank you for being real! To my MaBlack, Tekita: Words cannot express my appreciation for you. Thank you for being a part of my foundation and teaching me the reason why I minister (Luke 4:18). "What is the cost of your anointing?" I get it now. I love you. To my sister Tia: I love you so much. I miss our adventures. Thank you for every ride, prayer, fries with ice cream run, and all your love. To Trina: thank you for always encouraging me to "Bless Him!" I love you. To Dom: thank you so much for my pep talks when I was going through. Thank you for being an amazing example of a Godly Woman. To Elder Herbin: thank you for being an example of love. To Sandra Stovall and Krystina Smith, my burlap women, I love you for your continued support and realness. To my sixth grade teacher, Ms. Denita Dalton: the Harlem Renaissance woman in you inspired me to write. Continue to inspire as you teach. It's not in vain. I love you. To my Instragram and Facebook family: thank you for all the love and support. I appreciate you. To my haters: thanks for being my footstool and being there so that God could prepare this table for me.

IN
PURSUIT
OF ME

CONTENTS

EMPTINESS

Chapter 1

The Single Wife

I loved my marriage more than I loved my husband.

I remember sitting on the edge of my couch watching him pack his shit. My head and distraught face followed his every move as he paced back and forth to his car. I don't think I ever blinked. I felt my body moving back and forth as I sat in a dazed stupor; rocking to the same rhythm at which he paced. I contemplated begging him not to leave; saw myself dramatically crying to guilt him into staying but I never moved. I just stared, rocking back and forth. It was over before it was over so why couldn't I accept that it was over? When the door closed, finally, after the last trip, I broke down. "I can't do this," I whispered to myself. "I can't raise these kids, one with special needs, by myself. I can't do this. I can't manage this household by myself. I can't do this." I started to hyperventilate which led to a panic attack. This is the first time I contemplated suicide. "I. Can't. Do. This!" In one day, my happily ever after was snatched from me. The song I wrote for him three months after we got together, seven years ago, began to play in my mind; mocking me like a repetitious lullaby.

Where have you been all of my life?
With just one look into your eyes,
You left your mark right on my heart.
I'm going in circles trying to figure out,
There have been many
But you without a doubt are the one for me.
And that's why every star and every cloud
Reminds me of you
'Cause I see your face in all that I do.

I could no longer whimsically refer to "my husband" when conversing with fellow female peers and coworkers. There was no point in planning a hearty dinner if I did not have a man at home to enjoy it and smack me on my ass after he savored the first bite. And planning any future Saturday rendezvous, with complete itineraries for my family, were now null and void. What was I going to do now; separated from the man in whom I transitioned from adolescence to adulthood? Who was I? My hair was the length he wanted it to be. My mouth was never too slick in fear that he would be displeased and ignore me, but it was always slick enough to keep him pleased. My small waist sat on my wide hips just like he liked it. I never placed my feet anywhere that would cause him discomfort—or jealousy; rather, I was always walking on egg shells. Who was I? Without him, I didn't know. In what reason did I have to live?

I called him a thousand times that day in desperation.
It was exactly 9 days after he left. Father's Day.
Here we were, myself, and our two children with no father
to celebrate.
I wanted my husband to wake up on his back and smile down
at what I was doing to him.
And I would free my mouth to smile back at him and say

Happy Father's Day Daddy.
I wanted to cook him brunch and have our son serve him and say
Happy Father's Day Daddy.
He would feel proud to be a father and then recall me saying it first.
I called him a thousand times that day while our children slept in
our bed just after noon.
I lay calling in desperation in the middle of our son's twin size bed.
I felt so small in that bed as I sobbed pressing redial.
I always feel small when I cry.
I saw myself as tiny lying in the middle of that—
Hello?
Hello? I replied in a small voice.
Yeah?
You're supposed to be here, I sobbed.
Don't do this.
Did she cook you brunch? Did she tell you Happy Father's Day?
I asked in a dead pan voice.
Silence.
What are you talking about?
I swear you make me not want to live, I sobbed.
That's what you gone do. You gone do that to me.
Say you don't wanna live?
I sobbed harder.
Call disconnected.
I sobbed in the middle of that bed.
My son came in, tripped on something on the floor, fell,
shot right back up, and said I'm ok!
I looked at him with my tear stricken face and laughed.
He laughed back, temporarily calming my troubled heart.
I still don't know who disconnected the call.

For three months, I fell into a deep depression and lost a significant amount of weight. The weight loss was fine with me because I was on a mission to lose weight anyway. Before he left, I was a size eighteen. At the end of three months, I was a size twelve but I did not lose it in a healthy manner. My life is a complete blur when I try to think back to those days. I can't even remember those three months. What I do remember however, is running on auto-pilot. I would wake up, get my children ready for school and day care, go to work, pick them up, come home, feed them; what? I don't know. I don't remember cooking. There was no point. I don't remember eating. I had no appetite. I remember drinking cognac and consuming Hydrocodone that was prescribed for a toothache that was long gone to feel warm at night and masturbating to make sleep come easy. There were nights that I would lay in the middle of my bed, flat on my back, with tears rolling into my ears. I would sing the melancholy songs of my heart in a heavy timbre.

> *You stripped me of my dignity*
> *And crushed all of my self-esteem.*
> *I can't eat.*
> *I can't breathe.*

I would wake up with the sun shining on my face morning after morning. It was a constant reminder that it was a new day with me waking up to a harsh reality of the same bull shit.

A Sip of Wisdom

"A man can CAUSE you heartache. He can CAUSE you stress and pain but he can't COST you a damn thing; only you do that."
TiTi

One morning, I had an epiphany while writing in my journal: "I really miss him. I feel so alone. I miss how he used to..." I stopped because I didn't have anything to write. Here I was pining and depressed over a man that I did not even like? I was so depressed because I was focused on what my husband was doing. While lying in the bed all day while my children did God knows what, I would lurk on social networks to see how he was living. I would load my children into my car and show up where I knew he would be and on occasion, go to the house where he was living. That was *my* husband. He was *mine* and the thought of him with someone else literally drove me crazy. It was almost like he turned a light switch off when he left; like the past seven years meant nothing to him.

When he initially left I prayed for my marriage to be restored. I fought hard. However, the more and more he showed his ass, the less I prayed and fought. When the great epiphany came, I realized that I was fighting for something that he no longer wanted and the person he was showing himself to be, I didn't know. It was like he was a completely different person or was he this person all along?

I loved my marriage more than my husband. I think I was so blinded by my desire to be married with a family that I failed to really see who he was. He wasn't a bad guy. We just weren't compatible. Our futures and our dreams did not even coincide with each other. I made his dreams my dreams to preserve our relationship. Who was I? What about my dreams?

We forced our marriage. We had done everything else possible in a relationship: had two children, lived together, and seemingly, marriage was the next step to take. All we had were all these years as a foundation for our marriage, which weren't all that great might I add. The older generation was pushing us toward the aisle because we were living like we were married anyway. What was the difference? There was a big damn difference.

My husband proposed in April of 2010. Right before he proposed, I knew in my gut that he felt stuck in our relationship and had verbal confirmation that this was so. He had nowhere to go and nowhere out if he wanted to leave. He was stuck. I didn't want him to leave. I was in love with my life as a pseudo-wife and mother. I didn't know how to be anything else. I was also stuck.

We got married in April of 2011 and were separated by June of 2012. The contractual sanctity and finality of marriage was the big damn difference. I believed in it, wholeheartedly, even if our relationship proved to be a horrible foundation for a marriage. My biggest fear had occurred. I didn't want a divorce. I didn't want to be like everyone else in my family and society with multiple divorces.

I am not an advocate for divorce. I despise it. Even today, I wonder if I was supposed to keep praying and fighting to preserve our union. I wonder if I was supposed to just focus on me and learning who I was as a woman while interceding for my husband. He was having a quarter life crisis. Was I supposed to wait for him to come around? Now don't get me wrong, I have no desire to reconcile but I just feel that when people make the decision to get married, despite the circumstances, there has to be level of fight and loyalty to the decision that they made. However, in praying and fighting, I was quickly losing my peace of mind. It became harder and harder for me to accept that his behavior was a symptom of something deeper while he showed his ass. So I gave up. I have no regrets because now I am pursuing my dreams. It's almost scary to think that if I had not gone through that and the remainder of my story, I would not be pursuing me and my dream.

Besides being a wife and mother, I didn't know who I was and I so desperately wanted to find out. Who was I as a woman? I felt empty and incomplete. In my generation, we are all in pursuit of "something real" or our very own happily ever after to fill the empty space and complete us. I firmly believe that as a generation, we tend to chase after a happily ever after instead of making certain we know ourselves first and tackling our own issues before getting to know and taking on someone else's issues. I was devastated by the end of my happily ever after but once I realized that I was more in love with my marriage than my husband, I stopped moping around.

Initially, in my pursuit of me, I truly believe I lost my mind. I was free. No. You don't understand. I met my husband when I was 18 years old, had two children, and never really engaged in anything adventurous. I was now about to turn 25 years old and free. I had lost all this weight and was feeling rather confident.

I want you to ask yourself this: "What do I love about my significant other? What do I like about my significant other? Identify specific character traits. If you are racking your brain trying to answer, you may be in love with the relationship more than your significant other. Don't make the same mistake I did.

Chapter 2

The Morning After

Plan B: Hey You

I began to walk like I was feeling myself, got my hair cut in a bad pixie style, and I was eating. If you ever see me not eating, please know that there is something severely wrong. My style was conforming to the latest trends and I started to frequent the gym to take advantage of my recent weight loss. As I type this, the sheer realization that I possibly "let myself go" during my marriage is quite apparent. My love for cooking was rekindled. I was posting post workout pictures of my waist to hip ratio and cooking creations on social media to attract thirst. I mean let's just call it what it was. I was single. My husband was out doing him and it was time for me to do me.

I can still see myself lying across my bed. The children must have been asleep or with their father because I was having a moment to myself. Moments to myself are very rare. I was reading the latest issue of *Essence Magazine*. I saw my phone flash with a text message as I continued to read. It read "Hey You."

Don't ask me how this man got my number because I don't remember. Well that's the most I will divulge without exposing his identity. I started conversing with Hey You from that day forward. He was the epitome of the historical term, swag. He had it and he knew he had it. He kind of gave off the aura of the infamous character Marcus Graham from the movie *Boomerang*. He was pleasantly and disturbingly tall. Every time I opened my door, he filled the space completely. He took my mind off of my suppressed pain with his intellect and smooth tongue; and his smooth tongue. Our stories were the same—or he made his story reflect mine so it seemed the same. Game; either way we connected. He literally wooed my panties off of me. He was always there at night when I called. At night was when my loneliness really set in.

Ran into an old friend yesterday.
I was broken.
I was hurting.
He wooed me.
Said everything my husband never told me.
Told me he was coming to my house and hung up.
Game.
I started to send a text revoking my silent invitation.
I fought with my morals and values until I heard that knock on the door.
"When you open the door,
I want you to pull down your panties and let me suck on that pussy."
And I let him.
Because I wanted to feel better.

A Sip of Wisdom

Hey You was my sex buddy. My B.U.D.D.Y. as Musiq Soulchild so eloquently sung. Oh my goodness! I had a sex buddy; totally never saw myself having one but it happened. As I look back, I remember really smitten over this man. I talked about him all the time and the lust was real but we never would have made it in a relationship. He was just there at the right time. It was almost strategic the way he showed up. He showed up or I noticed him right after I had my great epiphany about my husband; right when I was supposed to be pursuing me. He temporarily filled the empty space in which my husband previously occupied. He got what he wanted which was to finally sleep with me. I got what I wanted which was to finally have my mind off of my husband and feel good.

Be careful about making those late night, "make me feel good" phone calls. Do not be fooled. You are still hurting and your healing is not in someone else. It will feel good temporarily but it will not last. This did not last and I ended up even more hurt.

The Morning After
Plan B: One Night Stand

I must have given One Night Stand my phone number while I was drunk a week earlier during homecoming. We were texting the night I officially cut off my "make me feel good" relationship with Hey You. Cutting him off hurt even though I knew nothing would come from it. I always have a difficult time cutting people off but I had to; our situation was too complex and I never saw myself settling in the role of anyone's sex buddy.

I was drunk and out with friends on this particular night. One Night Stand and I texted back and forth; with only a number popping up on my home screen to identify who he was. I didn't even know his name and was afraid to ask. How did One Night Stand end up where I was? I still don't know. I just remember feeling like I was doing me, for once. I ended up doing him and having my first one night stand; something, once again, I never ever saw myself doing.

Just got out of that relationship.
Doing me.
Doing things out of character to be noticed by him.
Thinking maybe he will realize what he lost.
Not doing me.
Doing him.
Went out.
Got drunk.
Got in another man's car.
Fell asleep in his arms, No.
No turned into Yes.
It felt so good.
I asked him,
In my drunken stupor

"How big are you?"
It felt good to be filled.
But I left empty.
Rode in silence back to my car.
Drove in shame back home.
Hurt me so bad.
Simultaneously sobbing and repenting.
Lost myself there,
For a moment.
Doing me.

A Sip of Wisdom

"The quickest way to get over a man is to get under one."
Somebody's Grandma

This is so shameful but I will be real. The only reason I know this man's name is because I saw it on his degree as I made my way to the bathroom to cleanse myself of our sex.

Because my husband was out doing him and I was hurt from cutting Hey You off, I wanted to do me. Even if that meant compromising my worth and placing my kids with multiple babysitters so I could go out and party. This was totally out of my character. As I stated earlier, I had gone out the weekend before this happened for homecoming. My children hadn't seen me consistently in two weeks, to include this occurrence. Technically, during the weekdays, I would go to work, pick them up from after-care, come home, cook dinner, and put them to bed. The weekend was supposed to be allocated for quality time with them. Here I was, basically neglecting them, as well as myself, to do me. I never have been the type to club or party but somehow I fell into the pattern of doing so. I like to go out every once in a while, specifically, once in a blue moon but I am more so of a "kickback at the house" type of person.

I was trying to keep up with my husband and mask the hurt from cutting off Hey You, all in my effort to do me. I went against all of my morals and standards while doing me! How does that work? Before you do you, really ask yourself: Who am I doing?

Chapter 3

Officially Unofficial

"Nah girl, we just talking!" Unknown

Yes. I sat my behind all the way down after that one night stand. I felt dirty and lost. You know what I felt like? Do you remember the scene in *Set It Off* when Jada Pinkett-Smith scrubbed her body after sleeping with that man for her brother's tuition money? Yep. That's exactly how I felt. As I type this, my stomach turns and a lump forms in my throat. I shocked myself. Who was I? Who had I turned into? I went from being a devoted wife and amazing mother to being a hoe in these streets (to my standards) all because my husband left me? I have very high morals and standards for myself. It all comes down to this rule of thumb for me: I never want two men in whom I have been intimate to be in the same place at the same time and be able to converse about me. One of my biggest fears is that my significant other will be in a barbershop where I am the topic of discussion. This is one of the reasons I do not sleep around but apparently I had thrown complete caution to the wind.

I remember driving home from the one nightstand and continuously shaking my head at how broken I was. I had to have been broken to do something like that because it was completely out of my character.

I grew up in church. I was the good girl in high school and when I had both of my children out of wed lock with my husband, I just turned into the imperfect good girl but I was still the good girl.

I have always felt like I was born in the wrong generation. I don't know if it's because my mother raised me by herself for the first nine years of my life and I was always in her mouth when her girlfriends came around or if God just made me like this. At age eleven, I knew all the words to the movie, *Waiting to Exhale*. In middle school, I would wear full suits with heels and at age sixteen, you could find me in my car blasting Lenny Williams' *'Cause I Love You* and Betty Wright's *Tonight Is The Night*. Who did I think I was? Heck if I know. How was I going to fit into this world?

I met my husband during my freshman year at Norfolk State University. While I should have been living out my glory days at a Historically Black College/ University, I was laid up under him, making babies. During my marriage, I lived vicariously through my peers, watching them transition in and out of relationships; hearing juicy stories of significant insignificant others. I could not understand the concept of a person talking and stressing over someone in whom they weren't in a relationship with. After listening to the ups and downs of these juicy stories, I would ask: "So, I mean, is this your boyfriend?" And the response would be an incredulous, "Nah girl, we just talking!"

What?! Can someone please tell me what the complete and total hell "Just Talking" means? So I found out that "Just Talking" is, apparently what my peers do to play the field in the dating game; but I was a one man woman. I would call my fellow peers for advice on dating and they advised me to just have fun. They explained that I had not lived yet and I was still young; basically saying it was ok to be a hoe for once in my life. But I did not have the time or the attention span to simultaneously, entertain multiple men; but I did and eventually only one piqued my interest.

I was asking advice of peers whose lives did not even mirror mine. I was a 25 year old separated and single mother. None of my friends had that life. They were either single and only responsible for themselves or married. I felt that no one could relate.

Never take advice from someone whose life you would not emulate.

My husband was acting crazy like he did not have as much responsibility to the two children we made together. I was so jealous because he was out just living as he pleased. I did not have the option as a mother to come and go as I pleased. His visitation schedule was limited to two hours on random days throughout the week because of his alleged living arrangements. I was pissed. He left and was winning because I was still living on his terms.

I was going to cook Thanksgiving dinner.
I couldn't afford to travel with two kids.
I was going to cook Thanksgiving dinner.
I stayed up all night prepping for dinner.
That's what my Mommie does.
I baked. I marinated. I chopped.
I sat on a stool with a trash bag in between my legs peeling sweet potatoes.
Feeling proud that I was slaving over these damn, stubborn sweet potatoes.
That's what my Mommie does.
I was making candied yams.
Then it hit me as I struggled to peel, I hate candied yams.
I threw the whole fucking sweet potato in the trash bag And the others followed.
I sobbed with my elbows on my knees and my face in my palms.
Candied yams were his favorite But he left 5 months ago...

Just call me the single wife.

My husband was stressing me out on a daily basis. I realized that the things he was doing were an indication of his character and I did not want that in my life. But I was still struggling with myself. Who was I? I still felt so empty.

I started praying and going back to church but I felt like God wasn't hearing me; like the silent tears every night and the moments at work when I had to close my eyes and breathe deeply just to keep it together were all in vain. I would go to church and the Word was completely irrelevant to what I was going through. If it was relevant, I was so angry at the series of unfortunate events that my life had sustained, that I could not hear it.

Eventually, after my husband recovered from his quarter life crisis and got his feet wet in the unmarried world, he came back stating that there was nothing out there for him. One night after a successful bout of co-parenting after taking our children out for our daughter's birthday, he tucked the children in and awkwardly waited around while I stood by the door for him to get the hint. He left. Then I received a phone call stating that he left his watch in our children's room. I went in the room to look for it and I didn't see it. I told him he could come back, even after the midnight hour, to look for it. I realized that he just wanted to talk and offered him a glass of wine.

We sat like strangers, in the dark with only the illumination from my candles lighting our way; he at the dining room table and me on my couch. He explained that he wanted his family back. I declined. He got upset stating that it was God's will for us to be together.

So let me get this straight, after inadvertently educating me on what the epitome of an asshole was for the past 6 months, he was back telling me what God wanted? I told him that he and God had horrible timing and both of them could get out of my house. Now, I repented because I will never get so far out of the will of God that I forget His power but, I never looked back.

A Sip of Wisdom

I was so consumed with what my husband was and was not doing, that I allowed his actions to affect my actions. The fact of the matter was he was going through his process and his process had nothing to do with mine. I went to my peers for advice and they insisted that I go out, date, and "do me." I was not ready. I was still hurting. In doing me, I neglected myself and my children.

I was empty and so desperately trying to fill that void. I was angry and I did not know who I was. I mean, there I was on Thanksgiving, separated from my husband and still preparing dinner as if he was there. In that moment, I realized that I had lost myself in my marriage. Instead of finding myself and healing, I hurt myself into different men and eventually someone else.

You are not ready. Be still. If you are a parent, please realize that your children need you now if not more than they ever have in their lives. They may be experiencing the same hurt as you. We often say that children are resilient but they hurt as well. They just display their hurt in different ways than we do; behavioral and/or emotional outbursts. You have to heal so that you can be healthy for them and yourself. Temporary fulfillment always masks wounds. If you are hurting, acknowledge the hurt. If you are angry, acknowledge the anger, be still, and heal. Don't hurt yourself into someone else like I did.

Chapter 4

Big Daddy

"It's all fun and games until someone gets their ass beat!"
Big Daddy

O r their heart broken. He piqued my interest. The conversation was easy. He didn't elude or ask me for a thing which made me want to give him everything; and I did, eventually, against my better judgment. We built somewhat of a friendship before getting serious. He never saw himself "talking" to someone with kids. There is that term again. He said I would be trouble and I told him I knew I was going to get my feelings hurt. In spite of our insight, we fell hard and I'm still trying to figure out how.

We were polar opposites; walking two different paths in life. Maybe we fell so hard because we needed each other in that moment in time. In the back of my mind, I felt like God had let me down, so man was the next best thing. I told him my story in brief synopsis form (I never completely open up to a man) and he wanted to be there for me. He told me his story and I wanted to make all his past wrongs, present rights. We needed each other.

Codependency

Anything I needed done, he did it or got it done. My Big Daddy. Anything he needed done, I did it or got it done. I never ask a man for anything. That was how I was raised. However, during our day to day conversation, needs would come up and they would mysteriously get met before I had a chance to do it on my own. He never went hungry or horny. He never went horny. I made sure of that. I was his comfort; always there when he needed reassurance, guidance, or just to rub his head—and his head. He always made me feel needed. I never felt needed in my marriage.

I would be lying if I said I wasn't happy. I felt like every relationship I endured built me for this moment with him. The potential he had inside of him was almost perfect for me but the reality was reality. He lived a fast life and mine was considerably slow. I tried to keep up the best I could, given my circumstances. Obtaining a babysitter for two children is not an easy feat but I wanted to be near him anyway I could. If that meant going to the club to flirt with him like we weren't an item, so be it. If it meant being up at 2:30 in the morning to discuss a loss and make it better with good head, so be it. I was up anyway because I was lonely. Even now, at this hour, I can smell the scent of alcohol, mixed with cologne, peppermint, and cigarette smoke. It disgusts and turns me on at the same time.

If it meant sneaking him out in the morning before my kids got up, so be it. If it meant my kids eventually meeting him during one of those mornings…

He said I would be trouble and I told him I was going to get my feelings hurt. I always know when someone stops feeling me. It's one of my greatest fears. When someone stops feeling me, the phone calls decrease, the passionate stares dwindle, and my needs aren't met; my need to be needed.

With one text message from her, I was no longer needed. The text messages led to dates and the dates led to lies. I always know when someone is lying to me. He didn't want to hurt me. I gather he felt stuck with the woman he said he never saw himself with because she had kids. I totally understood his disposition but my understanding did not change the fact that I had fallen. We were officially unofficial and he told me what it was in the very beginning no matter how far back the beginning was so he technically didn't cheat. I felt myself slip into the same depression that I endured after my separation but this depression was deeper. This time I bought black curtains to block the sunlight from shining on my reality in the morning.

I partially neglected my children. They were a constant reminder of why we couldn't be together. "I feel like you were made for me, except you met your husband first." "Those kids are supposed to be mine." "Everything is perfect until we get up in the morning." As I recollect those words, I can almost feel his strong hands on the small of my back crumbling my resolve as I reminded myself that my children come first. They were here before he was and they weren't going anywhere.

I hadn't fully healed from my separation therefore our end just added salt to a wound. My husband and I weren't friends. We never were. Big Daddy and I were friends, I think. I really don't know because I've never been friends with a male. He eventually knew everything about me and my cycle of hurt was repeating itself.

For the next several months, I would enter a whirlwind of dates, lies, needs not being met, sex to stay relevant, depression, worry, lurking, prayer for God to move Him because I wasn't strong enough to do it myself, nightmares of him and her, more prayers for the strength to cut it off, and finally clarity.

He was inside of me.
On top of me.
I craved this heat.
This warmth.

The proximity.
My Climax Began To Build.
He Was Almost There.
My heart POUNDED!
My
Lungs
Struggled
For
Air.
MyMindRaced!
ThisMomentRightHereIsEverything.
He'sWithMe.
NobodyDoesItLikeMe.
HeCameHomeToMeTho.
Right?ThisFeelsSoGood.
HeIsMINE.
Everything'sGoingToBeOk.
YEEEES!
I moaned as I let go of all inhibition and intuition.
Pushed out all warnings and negative thoughts.
My thighs trembled.
Drenched with his sweat.
Or my sweat. I do not know.
..."I love you girl."
Hot air on my ear as he whispered passionately.
The most passionate I've ever heard him say it
as he filled me with his apology
and confirmed it with a kiss to my neck.
My spot.
This is love.
But why do I feel so empty?
He rolled over and began to snore.
He apologized without actually apologizing
which warrants peaceful sleep.
I lay on my back, staring at the ceiling
as I felt a tear roll into the same ear in which he whispered,

mocking his words.
I fell into an unforgiving sleep with my face misconstrued.
This is the only love I've ever known from a man.
This WAS the only love I REQUIRED from a man...
"....Just let me make love to you. Let me make it right...."

A Sip of Wisdom

G od isn't going to move this one for you. There is a lesson in having to move the one you feel you cannot let go. Never settle for anything officially unofficial. Your relationships will only go as deep as your requirements and as high as your standards. At this point in my life, I had no requirements and I had no standards because I did not know myself. Big Daddy was a constant reminder that I had children at an early age. It wasn't his fault. This is the path I chose for myself and in my opinion he eventually felt stuck with me. What he said was true; he told me what it was in the beginning but I still held on, hoping for a happily ever after where he would love my children as I did and treat them as such. The fact of the matter was this: as long as I was running behind him, my children were being neglected, even if it was in the minutest way. When I couldn't run behind him, I was salty and not content with my life as a single parent. If I was going to be content with my life, I no longer could push myself to the capacity to pour into this relationship.

Today, we are going to stop pouring into relationships that do not pour into us. There are some relationships that we can pray about all day but until we take action, nothing will occur. I prayed so hard for God to move him; for God to help me get over him but I was still sticking around. I was pouring into the relationship even though it was not pouring back into me and I ended up empty, once again.

Stop pouring. Leave it alone. Stop looking at old pictures and text messages. Stop thinking he needs you in his life to be ok. Stop feeling like you are letting him down if you leave. You need you. Your dreams need you. Perhaps you stopped pouring into your goals and dreams. Perhaps you stopped pouring into your relationship with your children and true friends. Perhaps you stopped pouring into yourself.

It's time to heal. If I was going to heal, I knew I needed to look back at the pattern of relationships in which I had engaged in. I realized that I have always been in a relationship. Why couldn't I be alone for once in my life?

HALF EMPTY, HALF FULL

Chapter 5

Getting Back To Me

"Is the glass half full or half empty? It depends on whether you're pouring, or drinking." Bill Cosby

I suggest to you that there is a way to pour and drink at the same time. I loved my marriage more than I loved my husband and this, along with a combination of other factors, caused me to lose myself. But did I ever know myself?

Since I can remember, I have been empty, constantly attempting to fill the void. My mother and father departed ways when I was one year old. Therefore, I did not have a consistent, positive male figure during the most integral part of my life. Daddy issues create a void. The consistent, unwavering presence of a father or father figure is very imperative in a child's life because his purpose is to speak identity to his child. My mother is an amazing woman and parent who has always been there to speak identity over me but there is something about the presence of a man.

So I found myself attempting to fill the void. I remember journaling about feeling emptiness throughout adolescence. I went back and read my journals and found that I have always had a constant struggle of pleasing a man before pleasing God. I have always attempted to be the source of influence in every relationship I have ever participated in with a man. I was always the "good girl" who influenced or poured into them to be a better man but none of them had the true sustenance to pour into me. Therefore, I stayed empty, engaging in meaningless sex to keep them satisfied which caused a disconnect between me and God.

I examined the trend in the type of men I have attracted in the past; there is always a trend. My trend was that I attracted men who have lacked the influence of a mother in their lives. One was adopted, the other was abandoned by his mother at an early age, and two lacked a solid relationship with their mothers. Well what attracted them to me? I am very nurturing, a maternal quality and codependent, which means that I have a tendency to thrive on being needed by others. I was tired of this emptiness. I needed some direction.

Was your father consistently present during your childhood?
Yes or No (Circle One)

What trend do you notice in the type of men you attract?

A Sip of Wisdom

I wanted to be healed. I mean, I wanted to be healed last time but this time I wanted it badly. I was tired of being hurt and tired of being responsible for my own hurt. I could blame my husband and Big Daddy all day for the hurt I sustained but the fact of the matter is I knew what I was getting myself into. You know. That little tinge of hesitation is you knowing.

The last time I reached for God, I felt like He wasn't there. I prayed mediocre prayers—I just didn't want it bad enough last time. You have to want it bad enough. I needed a Word from God. I needed Him to be more than me saying my grace over my food and a gospel song on the radio. I needed Him to be more than the God I knew in my childhood. I wanted to hear His voice like I heard everyone else around me say they heard Him. If they could hear Him, so could I. I remembered hearing him clearly in my childhood and adolescence. I recalled a scripture that I learned while growing up: So then faith cometh by hearing, and hearing by the word of God, Romans 10:17 (King James Version).

The Word of God. This meant I needed to open my bible and actually read.

Anytime I read my bible, either I do not understand what I have read at all or I have a myriad of questions. I am just an inquisitive person as a whole. Do not be afraid to read your bible. Before you read, ask God to show you what He wants you to see. When you see something in the bible that piques your interest, do not be afraid to ask questions and research.

Chapter 6

MADE

Genesis 2 and 3, New Living Translation

O ne of my favorite shows to watch when I was a teenager was *MTV's MADE*. It was both hilarious and inspiring to watch people go through the process of being MADE into what they wanted to be. As I mentioned before, I was in love with the idea of marriage and having a husband more than the man my husband actually was. I strongly believe that because women want marriage and a husband so bad, we chase after men with the hope of fulfilling what we want.

As I reflect on what I have shared thus far, I have come to the conclusion that chasing men distracts us from becoming who we are, fully walking in our purpose, and ultimately being MADE for the role that we will be required to play in the marriage that we so desperately want.

I can't think of a time when I was not chasing after a man. I have always felt like I needed a man. It was almost like I did not feel complete without one. What was wrong with me?

So I began to read my bible for answers. I read through the first chapter of Genesis like blah blah blah and I got to the second chapter and was still like blah blah blah because we all know the story of Adam and Eve right? But there was one verse that stood out to me that caused me to go back and study these chapters more closely and by the time I finished, I was blown away:

> *Then the LORD God MADE a woman from the rib, and he brought her to the man (Genesis 2:22).*

Initially, the verse didn't pique my interest because of the word MADE but because of the rib being taken out of the man in the process of the woman being MADE. When I met my husband, he told me that he felt like he had finally found his rib. At the time I didn't know what that meant. I just knew it sounded deep and biblical. Yeah. He gamed me.

But anyway, these two chapters answered so many of my questions and I would like to share them with you:

Why do I feel like I *need* a man?

If you know the story of Adam and Eve and The Fall of Man, then you know that woman's curse because Eve ate the forbidden fruit is that we will have pain during child birth. But why didn't anyone tell us about the other half of that scripture? Look at Genesis 3:16.

If this is your first time opening a bible, don't feel bad. This was my first time opening my bible and actually understanding after being raised in church, so we're even. Try reading the *New Living Translation*. It is easier to understand.

You will see that the other half states, "And you will desire to control your husband, but he will rule over you."

I have learned, through my Bishop that the original Bible was primarily translated from the Hebrew language and that is why you will sometimes see different versions and translations of the Bible. With any translation, some words do not have equivalent meanings when translated to English.

Looking back at Genesis 3:16, you will see the word husband. Well I learned that in the Hebrew language, the word husband translates as Iysh which means man. Therefore, woman's curse because Eve ate the forbidden fruit is this: "I will sharpen the pain of your pregnancy, and in pain you will give birth and you will desire to control your husband (or *man*), but he will rule over you."

How can one control a husband or man without having one? Why do I feel like I need a man? Why do you feel like you need a man? Why do *we* feel like we need a man? Because of the curse, we have a natural desire for a man, a longing for a man to the extent that we settle to have one, in my opinion.

If we are not careful, a man we desire can rule over us; our thoughts, feelings, and emotions. At times, we can be so desperate to satisfy the longing to the point that we desire a man that has no authority and is not qualified to rule over us. Wasn't this the story of my life in the previous chapters?! The King James Version of that same scripture states, "and thy desire shall be to thy husband (or man)…" Why did God make *this* our curse? Perhaps the void and my emptiness were a set up from the beginning of time.

What caused Eve to eat the forbidden fruit?

Eve knew she wasn't supposed to eat the forbidden fruit so why did she? I had a really hard time figuring this one out but after some prayer, research, and putting myself in Eve's shoes, it became clearer.

Look at Genesis 3:1-6. There are a few very important things that I will to point out to you. Verse one says, "The serpent was the shrewdest of all the wild animals the LORD God had made…" If you look up the definition for the word shrewd you will see synonyms such as smart, intelligent, and clever.

You will also notice that the serpent appeared to be having a conversation *only* with Eve in verses 1-4. Where was Adam?! The last sentence in verse six almost seems to go out of its way to say, "Then she gave some to her husband, who was with her…" Who was with her? Where was Adam before when Eve was having this whole conversation with the serpent? I will reiterate that the serpent was smart, intelligent, and clever. He began a conversation with Eve only when Adam wasn't present.

What caused Eve to eat the forbidden fruit? Adam not being present and her need for tangible companionship. Because Adam was not present, the serpent stepped into the role of tangible companion. I say tangible companion because God was present, Eve just could not see Him. She could hear Him but she could not see Him. If she could hear Him, why didn't she converse with God in Adam's absence? The scripture does not say Adam and Eve saw God, rather it states that they heard Him (Genesis 3:8-9). Perhaps she wanted to speak with someone she could see and touch. Please understand that Adam's absence is not the only reason for Eve eating the forbidden fruit, but also that Eve didn't push past her need for tangible companionship and cling to God. He probably had some work for her to do on herself and in the garden but that's neither here nor there. Had she done this, she would not have been able to be distracted by the serpent.

You will discover as you read further, that my weakness and perhaps woman's weakness is that we desire tangible companionship. I desired tangible companionship even though God has been right here all along and I defaulted to tangible companionship when I felt alone.

The last thing I will point out to you is that Eve may have shared too much with the serpent. She talked too much. How many women do you know that talk too much? Not you. Women.

The serpent began to converse with Eve and she told him what God said which was over sharing (Genesis 3:2). If you notice, God is referred to as "The Lord God" after He created the heavens and the earth up until the serpent refers to Him as just "God". If you look up the word lord you will see that it means head or ruler. Eve repeated the serpent by referring to The Lord God as God. In doing this, she denounced God as head and ruler of her life. She also added to what God said. I believe this is when the serpent knew he could deceive her. Compare Genesis 2:17 and 3:3. You will notice in Genesis 3:3 that Eve added "…or even touch it…" God didn't say anything about touching the fruit. Had Adam been present, this would not have occurred.

How many times have we over shared with men to the point that we feel vulnerable enough to give our bodies to them? How many times have you shared your entire life story with a man and after, he comes off as sweet and understanding which makes you comfortable enough to sleep with him? Wasn't this the case with me and Hey You after my husband left?

What's so special about Adam being present?

Now this is the good part. This is where you learn the qualifications of a Godly man. Whether you are single or married, you need to know these qualifications. If you are single you need to know them so that you won't settle for any less after being MADE. If you are already married you need to know them so that you can spiritually influence your husband to meet these qualifications if he isn't already meeting them. Don't talk him to deaf about meeting them (1 Peter 3:1 NLT). Make sure you have been MADE first, then spiritually influence him to meet them. Just because you are a wife, doesn't mean you have been MADE. I can tell you that I didn't take the time to be MADE before I became a wife therefore, I was unable to spiritually influence my husband effectively.

Look at Genesis 2:4-7a, 15. You will see that God created or formed Adam from the ground after He saw that He had no one to cultivate the soil. God formed Adam from the ground to tend and watch over it.

If you look up the word tend you will see such synonyms as to take care of, care for, and minister to.

From this we learn that the first qualification of a Godly man is that he take care of, care for, and minister to the ground in which he lives (his house) and everything that lives in it.

The next thing that occurred was God breathing the breath of life into Adam's nostrils so that he could become a living person (Genesis 2:7b). Why did Adam need God to breathe into him? Well of course to live but I began to think about the job of the lungs in the human body. The lungs breathe in oxygen which is beneficial and release carbon dioxide which is waste. The lungs serve as a filter for what is beneficial and what is waste to the body.

From this we learn that the second qualification of a Godly man is that he stay connected to God so that he can discern and filter out what is beneficial and what is wasteful to the body (his, his family's, and The Body of Christ).

The next thing that happened in the garden really made me understand the importance and nature of man today. Look at Genesis 2:18, "Then the LORD God said, 'It is not good for the man to be alone. I will make a helper who is just right for him.'" Thereafter, God formed the animals and presented them to Adam so that he could name them or give identity to them. But after Adam named them, he still found that none of them were a "helper just right for him." We can examine this occurrence from two aspects:

1. When God allowed Adam to name each one of the animals, God gave Adam the power to give identity to that which He created.

What's so special about Adam being present? It is important for a man to be present to give identity and filter out waste. If he's not, the enemy (serpent) can come in and cause deception of identity, just like he did with Eve. Adam failed in his role to filter what the serpent was saying to Eve because he was not present. Because he was not present, Eve was able to exclude words and add to what God said which opened the door for the serpent to deceive her.

Ladies, is it not just like us to twist stuff around to make ourselves feel better about doing something wrong?

Just as it was imperative for Adam to be present, it is also imperative for a father to be present to give identity to his children, particularly his daughter. So many women are suffering with their identities because their fathers weren't present to give identity to that which God created. There are other instances where fathers are there yet still not present.

Please note that there is a huge difference between being THERE and PRESENT. So many men are THERE and not PRESENT. In order to be deemed present a man needs to be taking care of his home, filtering out waste, and exercising his power to give identity.

Perhaps not knowing myself and struggling with my identity were in direct correlation to my daddy issues.

From this we learn that the third qualification of a Godly man is that he be consistently present to exercise his God given power to give identity to that which God created.

2. I believe that God allowed Adam to name each one of the animals so that he would be able to determine exactly what a suitable helper for him was. Perhaps a man has to have a series of women presented to him so that he is able to determine what a suitable helper for him is when he finds her. Let me point out that I'm not saying that he has to try them out sexually to determine what a suitable helper for him is.

The greatest occurrence, besides woman being MADE of course, took place next: the deep sleep.

So the LORD God caused the man to fall into a deep sleep. While the man slept, the LORD God took out one of the man's ribs and closed up the opening. Then the LORD God made a woman from the rib, and he brought her to the man. "At last!" the man exclaimed. "This one is bone from my bone, and flesh from my flesh! She will be called 'woman,' because she was taken from 'man'" (Genesis 2:21-23).

Whoso findeth a wife findeth a good thing, and obtaineth favour of the Lord (Proverbs 18:22 KJV).

A man must spend undistracted time with God so that when God brings woman to him, he will be able to discern if she is his suitable helper and good thing.

From this we learn that the fourth qualification of a Godly man is that he be able to discern what a suitable helper for him is.

Now, back to being MADE.

When a man FINDS a wife, he FINDS a good thing.
It's not our job to convince a man that we are a good thing.
It is our job to be MADE and found.
After being MADE, if a man does not identify you as a suitable helper for him, either he has not been through the process that enables him to identify what is a suitable helper for him is or you were not MADE for him. Stop trying to force it if it's not it, move forward, and continue pursuing you and your purpose.

No matter how much it bothers me to admit it, because I'm still a little bitter, woman's primary purpose for being MADE was to be a "helper just right" for man. In addition to this, we also learn our role as women by the way Eve was made.

"Woman's greatest gift is not sexual power but influence."
Bishop Kim W. Brown

Eve was able to influence her husband to eat the fruit God specifically instructed him not to eat. In my research, I found that the reason Adam went against what God said was because he either didn't know which tree the fruit came from or he was distracted by Eve's body. Either way, had he been present he would have known.

Eve was MADE from Adam's rib. Ribs are part of the human body to protect internal vital organs. Eve failed in her role to protect her husband by appealing to his flesh on the outside, which she was not made to do. She was MADE from his rib to protect his spirit. That is why it is important to NOT default to influencing a man's body. I don't know why we think that giving a man our body is the way to bait him. It is not. In our generation, by the time we meet a man he has had multiple women presented to him in which he has most likely bedded into sexual partners. How do we show ourselves to be different? This is accomplished by helping and protecting his spirit. This is exactly what we were MADE to do; our purpose.

Please note that we were not only given the gift of influence to spiritually impact our men, but the world as well.

Because of The Fall of Man, we must be restored back to God and allow ourselves to be MADE by Him before even considering marriage. I am convinced that the Fall of Man was a set up authored by God so that He would once again be established Lord over our lives.

A Sip of Wisdom

S o we have learned that our curse is that our desire will be for a man and he will rule over us. We also learned that as women, we tend to desire tangible companionship and have a tendency to talk too much.

Our purpose, because of the way in which we were made shows that our greatest power is influence. Additionally, we have the ability to protect a man's spirit because we were made from his rib.

We should not be worried or consumed with the one God called us to protect, a Godly man, until we have allowed ourselves to be MADE by God. The result of being MADE is acknowledging the Lord God as head of our lives, knowing who we are, and learning how to fully walk in our purpose.

It bothers me immensely when we as women become immersed in preparing ourselves and our homes for our future husbands. It is perfectly fine to want a husband and aspire to marriage however; we cannot wait for our beloved to the degree that we are stagnant and settle. How many times have we wanted to wait or have waited for a man to get himself together? How many things have we put on hold in doing so? Ask yourself who am I and what is my purpose? We need to discover who we are, who God says we are, and walk in our purpose and power to influence.

The one God calls us to protect will be adequately managing the ground that God gave him to work and take care of. He will also be walking in his purpose, practicing his God-given power to give identity to that which God has created and already spoken to us.

This means we have to be restored to God before even thinking about a man giving identity to us. Open dialogue and true relationship with God must occur! Until we are restored to God, whatever identity a man gives will be foundation and validation; not confirmation of what God already spoke over and to us and what we have discovered within ourselves.

On too many occasions in our society, we jump into marriage with people with the intention of completing ourselves or filling the void. In our relationships, when the end is near, isn't it ironic how someone else steps in strategically to fill the void? It's almost like they are waiting in line, ready to fill the void as soon as the current relationship ends so that we don't even have an opportunity to feel the emptiness. Why is someone always there to fill the emptiness? Perhaps they are a distraction from what we really need.

The void or the emptiness was created to restore us to God first, so that we can know ourselves and our purpose in Him. Until that happens, every person will fail in filling the void.

Therefore, guard your heart. Ladies, be careful who you allow yourself to desire because in doing so, you give him the ability to rule over you. Is he qualified to rule over you? How does he manage the ground that God gave him? Is he working? Has he spent time with God so that he can discern what is wasteful and beneficial? Does he effectively walk in his God-given power to give identity to that which God created; you? Most importantly, do you know who you are first?

Are you still harboring old hurts from previous relationships? Fill your emptiness with God so that you can fall in love with Him, learn who you are, your purpose, and receive your healing.

I realized that if I was going to be healed and full, I needed to go back to my childhood and really analyze some things. I recommend that you grab a journal because I will be asking some thought provoking questions. Do not be afraid to be honest with yourself. Do not be afraid to write your feelings down. This is all for your healing.

I pray that my story brings about recognition in you and some of the things you have been through. I speak revelation and healing over you in the name of Jesus. Amen.

Chapter 7

Retrospectively Speaking

"The greatest gift God gave woman was not sexual power, but influence." Bishop K.W. Brown

I learned how to please a man at a very young age and the desire to want to please a man still haunts me today. It is really a love/hate thing and very hard to explain. In short, even though the smell of spit would bring the taste of vile to the back of my throat, I still would do whatever in my power to please my man, even neglect myself. This is the earliest account that I can recall a man placing a pull on me to please him. In addition to the curse, I believe the seeds were planted in this account.

All I know is if I tasted it again,
I would know the taste;
The raw taste of male pubescence.
Before I was even 5 years old,
I knew the taste.

He told me to put it in my mouth.
Sometimes when I see my son's underwear lying on the floor,
I remember.

Sexual abuse is very real and prevalent today. I think it always has been. My offender was very close in age and my mother took the necessary steps to protect me from it reoccurring however, it haunted me then and still haunts me today. In my childhood, I went about my life always needing to be touched. I can remember always needing physical stimulation even if that meant experimenting with friends; playing house.

In my marriage, occasionally during sex, and this is so difficult to share, I felt like I was being experimented on (I literally feel sick to my stomach as I write this). Of course there were times that I enjoyed it but those were only the times I was in control.

I absolutely, simultaneously love and hate for a man to look at me with desire. With that one ravishing look I feel powerless and powerful all at once. Powerless because I have always felt like men only appreciated my outer appearance and powerful because once he looked at me in that manner, I knew I had the power to conquer him just like my offender conquered me.

What is the earliest account that you can recall being the source of pleasure for someone, whether willingly or unwillingly?

Right after my first, real boyfriend's graduation.
We were in his truck.
His friend was asleep in the back seat
as we drove down the road while he fondled me between my legs.
"Can you...," He questioned as he looked down at his crotch.
My hand was already there.
I looked at him wide eyed.
"I mean if you scratch my back I'll scratch yours," He said.
I considered it and leaned over.
With my mouth full,

I repented in my head.
I never got my back scratched.

Can you recall your first account of giving and not receiving in a relationship?

I can. Mine was when I began the tug of war of pleasing God and pleasing man. I was 15 years old and you could not tell me I wasn't in love. Okay? When he asked, I couldn't say no because I didn't want him to stop liking me. Wow. I gave this man oral sex with his friend in the back seat who was allegedly asleep because I didn't want him to stop liking me. As I type this, all I can do is shake my head and laugh shamefully at my naivety and stupidity.

I was not myself in this relationship. This is the relationship in which I went on my first date. I ordered a quesadilla feigning lack of hunger and I didn't even finish that. I was starving and trying to be cute. He talked incessantly about his ex-girlfriend in detail and I giggled after each remark. I really was pissed and jealous. While we conversed in person it seemed like he looked past my words and was deafened by his desire for my body. I don't remember much else regarding this account except the ultimate heartbreak but then that would be another sad love song.

I do remember this: a couple of days later, after the graduation, we had Monday night prayer at my church. Monday night prayer was when our congregation would gather and the ministers of the church would intercede over the house. To say that I was all to pieces would be an understatement. I sat in shame repenting and begging God to forgive me in my seat. While everyone stood, I sat. I was so heavy. My pastor called me on the microphone and my whole body ran hot like it does when you see those blue flashing lights behind you while driving. Did God tell her what I did? Oh my God! I walked to the pulpit on legs the consistency of cooked angel hair pasta.

When I finally reached her, she said one word: pray. I took the microphone and did just that. I don't remember what came out of my mouth. I just prayed, being led by God. This blew my entire mind! God wanted me to pray over His house? Here I stood using the same mouth to pray as God called and led me. In that moment I knew that God loved me in spite of myself but this realization was not enough for me to totally surrender to Him.

A Sip of Wisdom

E very horrible thing you have experienced will be turned around to free you and the people you knowingly and unknowingly influence. God's master plan is taking course.

Let's be real: Sometimes it's hard to go to God because we low key, sometimes, blame Him for the mess we have been through:

Molestation
Abandonment
Loss
Sexual Abuse
Rejection
Domestic Violence
Physical Abuse
Emotional Abuse
Verbal Abuse
Identity Issues
Mental Health Issues
Dysfunctional Relationships
Codependency

You may not want to hear this but all things are working together for your good. Try to remember that everything you have been through, whether it was by your doing or not, was a set up to restore you to God and in turn, mold you for your purpose in life.

I encourage you to identify everything you have experienced and share it with God. If you have to, highlight or circle what you have been through or add to my list. Tell Him how you feel about it. You can go to God concerning anything. You do not have to speak in an eloquent way, just talk to Him. If you have a hard time talking to Him, because it can feel awkward, write it down.

Your body is still a temple, Beautiful.
I don't care if you have offered it or it has been taken,
it is still a temple.
You may feel like since you have tainted your temple,
you might as well give that part of you versus your heart, soul, and mind.
In turn, that validates and strokes your ego temporarily.
It gives you power over that which you feel
took your power in the first place.
Your vagina is not your virtue.
Every woman has a vagina,
but no one has the same make up as your heart, soul, and mind.
You have more to offer.
You have more to offer than what you are offering.
And it's not because you don't know what you have to offer,
you just use what gets you quick results.

Retrospectively Speaking

"Hindsight explains the injury that foresight would have prevented." Unknown

My high school sweetheart; I wanted to help this boy so bad. He had been abandoned at an early age. I knew in my gut that the relationship was not right. My intuition told me and God told me very candidly. I was in leadership at my church and this relationship was so taxing because I was trying to be there for him and please God. I would do whatever in my power to keep him happy because I did not want him to think I abandoned him as well. He was broken. I wanted to fix him but I was blind and broken as well.

At the cinema viewing the Ray Charles movie,
making out with my high school sweetheart
and somehow between the heated teenage exchange,
I looked up while he grabbed the inside of my thigh.
Scene on the screen was Ray wandering blindly
through the sheets on the clothes lines
and I heard,
even on top of my false moans
as I turned to looked him square in the eye:
"Do you see your future in his eyes?"
I saw nothing.
In my mind,
I told God no.
"You are wasting my time and his." God replied.

I remember hearing God so clearly that day. I don't remember the rest of the movie and I have no desire to see it again.

Are you currently participating in a relationship in which you know in your gut is not right? Has God spoken to you about your relationship? What is keeping you from adhering to your intuition and/or Him?

A dream:

It was a beautiful afternoon. The sun was shining.
I was in my car. Alone.
I remember smiling.
That type of smile you feel in your soul.
The windows were down. Breeze in my hair.
I proceeded to get on the interstate on the on ramp which was a sharp turn.
I saw myself smiling as I smoothly entered ongoing traffic.
I kept driving toward the sun.

Next scene, same dream:

It was a beautiful afternoon. The sun was shining.
I was in my car with my husband as he drove.
My face was emotionless as I looked out of my window.
The windows were up. The car was stuffy.
He exited the interstate in a hurried fashion.
I felt the car lose control. My head snapped forward.
My eyes grew with fear. My head snapped to look at him.
His gaze was forward and emotionless
even in the midst of my panic
as we fell past the guard rail.

I woke up:

And snuggled closer to him for comfort while he slept peacefully.

I have learned that God tends to speak to me through my dreams. I had this dream during the early stages of my relationship with my husband after we moved in together. The interstate that was featured in my dream is literally down the street from our first apartment. I smile when I drive past it in recognition. It's almost like God and I have a loving "I told you so" moment when I drive past interstate VA-168. God warned me of the heartache I shared with you in chapter one, five years before we separated; even before we got pregnant with our first child and got married.

So once again I ask, has God spoken to you about your relationship? What is keeping you from adhering to your intuition and/or Him?

A Sip of Wisdom

I have never not been in a relationship. The last three accounts I shared were over a three year span before meeting my husband at age 18. Going back and really analyzing each encounter was very necessary for me and I hope it has been for you. It made me realize that someone has always been there to fill my emptiness. Revisiting my molestation was very difficult but it is the root of my relationship patterns and the foundation of how I see and display myself. Each encounter was indicative of one very apparent notion: I was codependent.

I had to feel needed and when I did not feel needed I would do what I had to do to remind my man that he needed me and I needed him. If it meant ignoring phone calls until he thought I was doing God knows what, I would do it. If it meant dumbing myself down so that he felt smarter, I would do it. If it meant posting a picture on a social network that was a bit risqué to make him question my intentions, I would do it. If it meant acting weak and magnifying my every day stress, that I could handle before he came along to the point where is seemed that it was more than I could bear just so he would step into the role of man and comfort me, I would do it.

Are you codependent?

Chapter 8

Codependency

A stronghold is not a stronghold because it has a hold on you but because you have a strong hold on it.

C odependency; I cannot type that word without shaking my head and smiling knowingly. Codependency is my stronghold. I sat down and thought about it and my stronghold is not so much having a man as it is codependency. However, a man plays a significant role in it because that is where my void is. There is something about a man being there. No. It goes beyond that. There is something about a man being present. Being present, in my opinion, is so much more than being there. I have never experienced an ever present man in my life. What is being present? A man is present when he exercises his God-given authority to speak identity into that which God created and he filters anything out that goes against that which God created and that which he spoke. That was a mouth full so let me break it down for me and you. I am referring to when I spoke about Adam. Adam's weakness in the garden of Eden was that he was not present and because he was not present he could not speak true identity to what the serpent said and to what Eve saw the fruit to be (Genesis 3:6).

The fact of the matter is this: Due to several life circumstances such as my father not being present, what I was lacking was identity and as a result of that I became codependent.

Codependency, as defined by me, is when one feeds, gets off on, or is fulfilled by pleasing and being needed by others. Codependency has been the story of my life as you have read thus far. As I stated, I am a nurturer. I believe that I have a gift for nurturing. I love to care for people and make them smile. Pleasing people makes me smile. Now, there is nothing wrong with that as long as people are making you smile as well. There is nothing wrong with pouring into people as long as they pour into you.

My process began, once again (this has been an ongoing cycle with me), when I went to God raw and tired. I remember feeling empty because I had poured so much of myself into my marriage and husband. I also felt abandoned. I remember being so angry. In retrospect, I wonder if I was angrier because of my own childhood issues rather than him leaving. He was leaving me like everyone else. Was it fair for me to put all of that on him? I really had a deeper healing that needed to occur.

My God, I remember being so angry. I would think about him not being there then my thoughts would gravitate to my father not necessarily being physically present when I needed him. I always felt like my father did not KNOW me. I remember being excited to see him but when I arrived at his house I always felt empty because he did not know me. Just like I have felt in the presence of every man in whom I have been in a relationship because I didn't know me. I held on for the sake of them just being physically there, avoiding the emptiness; the void.

I went to God requesting that He fill the void and I began to get closer to him. I began to fall back in love with my very First Love. I began getting back to me; being content about my life and in who I was. Guess what came next? Yes, a distraction; another man right when times got hard.

Big Daddy came along when I was going through the stress of my divorce and learning how to co-parent with my ex-husband. Instead of clinging to God and going to Him for comfort, I reverted to my place of security; a man, tangible companionship. I notice now in my life, when things start to go wrong, I automatically start to feel lonely; like I need a man.

My distraction was almost perfect. Big Daddy gave me exactly what I wanted; things that I never received in my marriage. The enemy is crafty! I never felt needed in my marriage. Big Daddy needed me. He valued my opinion. He needed me; music to a codependent's ears. My past relationships have only fed me because I had someone who needed me. I was taught how to please a man at an early age and they loved it. At the end of the day, after being needed and pleasing, I was still empty, uncomfortable, and unloved. The only comfort and love I have ever known with a man has been through a man appreciating my body, engaging in sex, and pleasing him.

The downfall of my relationship with Big Daddy stripped me of everything I knew about myself and made me question myself as a woman. It made me question my beauty, my purpose, and who I was. I questioned myself because I still did not know who I was. In my bitterness, I began to think to myself: "I don't need a man. I'm going to get back to me." I started to pursue me and I realized that I was still empty and still hurting.

Therefore, I went to God raw, tired, fatigued, and begging for His love and strength again. He told me to pursue Him and in Him I would find me; In Pursuit of Me.

A Sip of Wisdom

The ultimate finding after surrendering and having the opportunity to fall in love with Christ is not a significant other. There is this growing trend where people are taught that if we surrender to God and complete the assignment He has given us, our significant other will find us. We cannot wholeheartedly focus on our assignments if we are always looking for a significant other in our peripherals. As a result, we fantasize about this happily ever after of a significant other finding us to a point of distraction.

Who are you? Pursue you.

.

Chapter 9

In Pursuit Of Me

Me Time: Poetry and Prose

When I say in pursuit of me...
No I'm not trying to find myself.
I am myself.
I know what gifts I possess.
I know what pisses me off.
I know what makes me smile.
I am in pursuit of me.
I am cultivating my gifts.
I am making me smile.
I am wooing myself so that I know what it feels like
and I'm not wowed when someone else is just scratching the surface.
I'm setting the standard for myself.
This is what I deserve.

"She is beautiful, and therefore to be wooed; She is a woman, therefore to be won." William Shakespeare

I decided that I would woo myself and get some standards and expectations. What are ways you can woo yourself today? Set some standards and expectations. Write them down.

In pursuit of me.

I met me the other day.

I caught my eye.

Piqued my interest.

I had this thing about me that compelled me to....

Can I talk to me? I really wanna know my name.

I just have to know me; what makes me tic?

What makes me smile from my soul?

What is my favorite whatever?

I wanna know what turns me on so I can be all that and more.

What stimulates my mind?

What makes my heart flutter?

What makes my thighs clench?

I have to give me, me.

Until I'm full.

Until validation is obsolete.

Until I admire who I see in the mirror.

Until I'm in love with me and every characteristic that makes me, me.

Every facet that deems me authentically me.

I cannot cultivate me in anyone else but me.

Write down your favorite everything; color, drink, activity, hobby, stress reliever, movie, song, and so on.

Now go back through the list and cross out anything that you thought was your favorite but realized it was someone else's favorite that you adopted.

Looked up and wine was poured; favorite kind.
Candles were lit.
Lights were off.
Bath water drawn.
Water just right.
Bubbles were plentiful.
Slipped in.
Playlist started; Maxwell, Will, Al, Anthony, Lalah and John....
Candlelight bounced off pretty brown skin.
Felt fingers in my hair.
Eyes closed.
Plush wash cloth moved up my thigh.
Sighed.
Warm water trickled down my back.
Hissed.
Terry cloth massaged me dry.
Oil kissed my skin.
Executed just right.
By me.

Pamper yourself tonight. Pick up your favorite beverage. Pay attention to yourself. Light some candles. Do your nails and toes. Run yourself a bubble bath and enjoy what makes you, you.

If you do not have anyone;
One person you call friend or one person in whom you can rely,
don't sit there and harp on it.
Be that person for yourself!
Be the person you want in your life.
Do the things you crave for others to do for you, for yourself.
That way you know how it feels to be treated nice to your own standard and
when people come along to pursue you,
you are not so easily impressed.
You are a prize and a gem.

I remember having an argument with my husband where I raved about how when I go to the store, I always think about him by buying his favorite snacks. There was one time he went to a particular restaurant and did not think to bring me back a piece of chocolate cake. I was upset and acted as such. This was a little childish but you get the point.
If you want some cake, go buy yourself some and stop sulking about the fact that someone didn't get you some.

Warm it up. Get yourself a scoop of vanilla bean ice cream and strategically place it on top of that warm chocolate cake. Then, watch with anticipation as the ice cream melts a little. Get yourself a spoon and attack it slowly.

Do these things for yourself so that when someone comes along you won't glorify him doing less than what you deserve.

Pick up your favorite snack and enjoy it tonight. Slowly.

A Sip of Wisdom

I had the opportunity to visit Richmond for a friend's graduation. Before I got back on the road to go home, I decided to visit Carytown and I fell in love. I walked the streets and enjoyed different foods. I bought little trinkets from vendors and had the opportunity to write.

From my journal: *"For the first time in my life, I am single. No boyfriend, no husband, no officially unofficial, and no potentials. I am happy and it means the whole wide world to me; being healed from all pain and I'm free. I will be real, I have my moments where I crave companionship but one thing that has remained the same with me is that I enjoy my own company. I love being solo. I'm an introvert at heart. I learned that as a mother and social worker, mental health is everything. Therefore, I take time to myself when I can.*

1. Whether in a relationship or not, I encourage you to have moments when you can enjoy you. Stop being overwhelmed by the notion that you cannot afford a vacation. Go to a neighboring city and explore. Eat something different. Browse in specialty shops. Enjoy the sound of no one calling you by name or title. Enjoy the wind on your skin.

2. Stop focusing on the fact that you have no one to share it with and share it with you. You miss you. You need you. You can't heal in someone else. You are great company."

I remember feeling so beautiful on this day. I was content and had no issue with walking down that street alone. The wind was a gentle reminder that God was right there with me. He was restoring my confidence and teaching me who I was as a woman. I know this sounds weird but I felt like I was getting my sexy back; like He was restoring my swag—But you know this wouldn't be my life if there wasn't another distraction or two right?

Chapter 10

Distractions

"Distractions diss your traction and are meant to get you off track."
Bishop K.W. Brown

Have you ever had someone slide in your life at the right time? I mean, it was technically the wrong time because I was just getting back on track, learning about the gifts God gave me, and discovering who I was but it was *so* right to me. I mean he was gorgeous. He made me question whether God places people in your life so that you can learn certain lessons or if the enemy places people in your life and God decides He's going to the glory from the situation if you fall prey to the distraction. Either way, I fell prey to the distraction and struggled.

Whatever your gifts are,
linked with overcoming your struggle,
will equal your purpose.
Your Gifts + Overcoming your Struggle = Your Purpose

What are your gifts? What are your struggles? Write them down.

One of my gifts is obviously writing and My Struggle was gorgeous. Let's call him My Struggle. I inadvertently learned so much from my experience with him. He confirmed that I struggle with putting a man in the place of God. He also made me recognize that so many other women do this. From that I realized that my purpose was to overcome my struggle and influence other women to do the same.

But wait, did I mention that he was gorgeous? I'm pretty sure I did but just in case I didn't, he was gorgeous. I asked him how tall he was and his answer, alone, made my thighs clenched. He was 6'5. I know. Your thighs just clenched too. He had this scruffy, preppy thing going on which is my complete weakness. Imagine this: a Mohawk, a pair of designer eye glasses, and his lips; they made my thighs clench as well. His lips were surrounded by a scruffy yet well groomed beard and the end of it grazed his precisely tied eclectic bow tie. I have a thing for contrasts and this man screamed contrasts. For example, I like educated thugs; thugs with Master's degrees. I like men who love Jesus, but give a slight indication that they will set it off or have in the past; men of Purpose.

We clicked so well. His spirit and intellect were so refreshing. He was like the male version of me; which means I saw many similarities between us. We will talk about that in one second but let's talk about how gorgeous he was and how he treated me. This man wined and dined me, paid attention to detail; gosh darn it, he almost wooed my draws off of me with his spirit and intellect alone. He listened to me, encouraged me, and his words were always on time. For the first time in my life, I was turned on by a man's intellect and it did not help that he was gorgeous. So I had to take a vow of celibacy. I know it's a bit extreme but I knew if I did not take this vow, I was going to sleep with this man and it was going to be too good. I was going to get caught up once again and I had come way too far.

> *I want him so bad.*
> *To just please him.*
> *To put my mark on him.*
> *To just have him look up or down at me like what are you doing to me.*
> *To satisfy my need to please.*
> *To satisfy my need to validate the fact that I'm a woman.*
> *I'm so lonely.*
> *I feel so alone.*
> *Can I just lay up under him?*
> *I just want to feel that…*
> *That*
> *Connection.*

I wanted him however, I realized that after writing the previous piece that I still wanted to default to use sex to bait him and connect with him. I was craving a connection more than I was craving sex which was primarily my reason for deciding to be celibate. Sex was no longer how I wanted to connect with a man. This is when I told him my whole life story and ended it with "I cannot disappoint God this time. I have to pass this test."

When I met him and we initially conversed, it was apparent that he had gone through and seemingly come out of what I already had. We concluded that we were beneficial to each other because we could exchange past situations and testimonies. I told him I only wanted to be friends and by friends I meant strictly platonic because I realized that he was placed in my life as a distraction. I don't know why I felt like I could be friends with this man because I have never been friends on a platonic level with a man, ever.

Although I feel his effort decreased, he understood my celibacy and continued to be there for me. My Struggle gave me exactly what Big Daddy did not: he poured into me which made me want to make him my refuge. He was filling my emptiness. It made me want to go to him with all of my issues just so he could tell me it would be ok. The only person I wanted to be my refuge and fill my emptiness at this point was God. I fought hard because I was trying my best not to put anyone in God's place. I had done that way too many times. I knew that I needed to make God my refuge. He is a jealous God and I knew for once in my life I needed to make God my everything.

I asked God what his purpose was and I heard one word: distraction. I went to church after hearing what God said and my Bishop preached on distractions. Let me tell you how I twisted the revelation that God gave my Bishop around to validate me not cutting this man off because he was my distraction and My Struggle.

It was my mindset that I would keep My Struggle around, conquer the distraction, and give God the glory when I did. I was a mess. Why did I think I was strong enough to keep My Struggle around? We went out and our chemistry was out of this world. I wanted to just hand him my panties at that restaurant. Don't judge me. I saw similarities between us in that we struggled with the same stronghold: codependency. Because I recognized that, I wanted to fix him, with my codependent and broken self.

There is always a pull from each person when two people are attracted to each other. In most cases where there is a fixer and a broken person, the broken person has the greater pull because the fixer is just as broken.

I was struggling with physical attraction, trying to be an influence in this man's life, and pleasing God. I was in no place to influence him because technically, I was right where he was if not a couple of steps behind. I also could not be consistent with my own standards to save my life.

I struggled between sending him pictures of my body and screenshots of my morning devotions.

I found myself in my newly purchased bathing suit.
I started to send a picture to My Struggle to get his approval.
I just wanted him to say it looked good. Why did I need him to say that?

I wanted his approval just like a little girl exhibits behavior to simply say:
"Look Daddy" for his approval.
There go my daddy issues again.
They have turned me into an attention seeking woman.

Are you an attention seeking person?

I would send him a picture, immediately get convicted, and have to apologize instead of just not sending it in the first place. I fought with myself on whether to send him a nasty text message or the Word I *thought* God gave me for him. I was a mess.

A Sip of Wisdom

The more we conversed the harder I fell and that was not what I wanted. I just wanted him to be my friend without the added feelings. I recognized that I was not ready for a relationship but it was almost like I could not help it. After every conversation, I found myself struggling with my feelings even more. I had to fall back and focus on my purpose and assignment. I had come way too far to completely get off track so I fasted to stay focused and he was part of my fast. I always fast when I need to regain my focus. My fasts normally consist of making certain my mind is averted to God whenever I think about what I'm not supposed to be thinking about; in this case, My Struggle.

As a result, I went missing in action. I cut our conversation short without any notice. It wasn't fair to him but I had to. He reminded me that I was still broken and codependent. I told him as such. I had lost focus and I had diminished my worth as a woman once again to keep the attention of a man.

I cannot expect someone to know my worth if I do not know it myself. My worth is not diminished because one does not recognize I am priceless. My worth however is tarnished when I do not recognize I am priceless.

I was still broken and a mess. Had I considered that I wasn't ready to date; that I just wasn't ready to deal with someone else because I hadn't really dealt with me.

Distractions
Integrity is when your public words line up with your private life.

M y Struggle was an extremely gifted and talented man. It was apparent that he had a call on his life. He was simultaneously walking in his call and his struggle. Aren't we all? I was no different but I wanted to be a woman of integrity. I had already messed over my call once in my life.

Growing up in church,
we master the imitation of a relationship with God.
We learn how to praise, pray, preach, and worship
just like whomever we admire (man).
We begin to live right in public so that we do not disappoint whoever we
admire or are held accountable.
But what are we doing behind closed doors?
We get to a point where we reach God to be prepared.
Where we scratch God to feel good.
Where we skim God just to keep our light bright so that people can see.
But we never truly KNOW Him.
It's almost like He is beside us but not IN us.
What happens when man lets us down or we are exposed?
We transfer the disappointment to God
and hide from Him
because in fact we have made man our god.

Very few people know that I was a full blown deacon at age 17, like a real one; on the board with the old people. I also was a youth leader of a very large church. At that time, my whole leadership role was based on pleasing people. I knew God but I didn't truly know Him; know Him to the point where I cared if I hurt Him. I went to my leader and told her that I wanted to sit down from ministry stating that it was too strenuous with me entering college. I was really having sex with my now ex-husband every day, all day. Right after I sat down, I got pregnant. I felt like I let so many people down, especially the young people I was influencing. I could not make the same mistake again.

I looked back over my life and realized that even after I got pregnant God still told me he would take care of me. He did just that even in the midst of my mess. My ex-husband and I lived together for 5 years, had two children out of wed-lock, and God still supplied every need. I'm not highlighting my sin. I'm just explaining how faithful God has been as a foundation for me to reiterate that I could not let Him down this time.

A Sip of Wisdom

"I'm calling you to a deeper relationship with Me; where you walk with Me and talk with Me and I begin to tell you how you are My own; a relationship where you hold My hand and walk by faith. Just trust Me. Believe Me. I have delivered you countless times when you weren't doing right. You do not have to be perfect. I know who you are. I know who you are not. Just talk to Me. Before you panic, talk to Me. When you're excited, talk to Me. When you're over it, talk to Me. I'm here. I love you and desire to see you do well. Let Me show you My love. Let Me love you until you fall in love with Me. Until you profess your love for Me not only in words but in your actions as well."

Love,
God

Chapter 11

Surrender

Don't go back. Stop avoiding the process. You are stunting your growth. Your personal freedom and direction for your purpose, assignment, and dreams are in the process.

In 11 years, since age 16 years old, I have never not been in a relationship. My pattern has been that when a relationship ends, I write for release and begin a retrospective process like the one you read about in chapter seven. Right when I begin to focus on me (and normally that involves a lot of writing), I allow myself to be distracted by another man and before I know it, I'm in another relationship. I have started approximately 3-4 journals after each break-up I have encountered over a course of 11 years. The great realization is that this book has possibly been started 3-4 times but each time I got caught up in someone else and would hold on to the relationship even though it caused me to struggle with who I was and my purpose.

I'll explain. I transitioned from adolescence into adulthood with pleasing a man as my main focus, so much so that I was academically suspended for not making higher education my top priority as I should have. Before I knew it I had two children. Thank you Jesus for them because they are the only reason I was motivated to complete my bachelor's degree. I had to be an example for them. Now I had a whole family and career in which I had to focus. My identity was molded into being a wife and a mother but who was I as a woman? If those roles were stripped from me, who would I be? If your current roles were stripped from you, whether by will or not, who would you be as a woman? The role of wife had been stripped from me and I realized that I didn't know who I was. I felt like my ex-husband took who I was with him. While in the process of learning who I was, I met Big Daddy and My Struggle and started to repeat the pattern. How was I going to be free?

First, I needed Jesus and secondly, I needed to know who I was. My codependency was hindering me from focusing on what I needed and what I was destined to accomplish. I noticed that right when I surrender to God, a distraction is strategically sent to get me off track. Normally the distraction is an unfortunate event that causes me to seek comfort; a bill due, work stress; you name it. I go to men for comfort and tangible companionship and in doing so, stunt my growth. Instead of seeking God for comfort and His companionship, putting my worries in His hands, and just figuring it out, my first instinct is to call a man to feel good.

Do you know how many times I wanted to call My Struggle? At that moment, I would have expressed how taxing this process has been and he would have told me that everything was going to be alright. The deep, baritone raspiness of his voice was all I wanted to comfort me but I didn't call him because I was tired of falling into the ongoing pattern of using a man for comfort and putting a man before God.

Comfort is a distraction.
Stop using what is comfortable to you,
To distract you from the process.

The fact of the matter is this: if I do not write, I do not feel relief from my inner turmoil. For me, writing is a form of communication with God. When I write, it's almost like I'm pouring out my feelings and at the end, God gives me the lesson I am supposed to learn. The only time I cannot write and hear from God clearly is when I am distracted. When I am distracted I start to sin in some form or fashion, beat myself up about sinning, and I hide from God in shame.

A Sip of Wisdom

I do not regret anything I have experienced because I am wise enough to know that it was all a part of my journey and this testimony. God has carried me and been my protection through a great deal and variety of situations. He has equipped me with the gift of writing to share and free others. Do not allow the enemy to make you live in shame and shut you up. You are not stuck in your struggle. God is going to use your gifts to free you and others in the name of Jesus, Amen.

The Filling

Chapter 12

Hey Thirsty

John 4:1-42, New Living Translation

The aforementioned fast occurred during the week of Resurrection Sunday. I attempted to eliminate all distractions and placed myself in isolation to regain my focus. God instructed me to read several different passages of scripture. This particular passage of scripture about this woman would change my life forever because I found that the bible described this woman to be what we call today; a THOT. I know it's a bit much but just keep reading.

Why did the Samaritan woman choose the hottest time of day to fetch water?

The scripture makes note that it was noon when she met a tired, hungry, and thirsty Jesus at the well. Please understand that although Jesus was wholly spirit He was also wholly flesh because of how He was made. God sent His spirit to impregnate the Virgin Mary; flesh.

Jesus was tired because He took the long way through Samaria to get to Galilee. Research shows that the other women in her village fetched water early in the morning because it wasn't as hot and so that they would have it to fulfill their duties throughout the day. A thirsty Jesus asked the Samaritan Woman for water and in doing so broke 3 rules: He, a Jew, spoke to a Samaritan, He spoke to a woman in public, and He gave the notion that He was going to drink from her jar which would have made Him unclean.

Jesus offers the woman Living Water so that she will never thirst again and she replies earnestly, stating that she indeed would love the Living Water so she never would have to come back to the well again. What was up with her and this well and what did Jesus mean by Living Water? She did not understand what Jesus was talking about so He broke it down for her. I believe she was a visual learner like me. So He got her all excited about the Living Water and told her to go get her husband. The woman replied (after she picked her face up off the ground) that she did not have a husband. Jesus in turn told her that historically she had five husbands and at that current time she was living with a man that was not her husband. Dang Jesus! He came for her life. No literally. It gets better.

What also intrigued me about this woman is that nowhere in this passage will you find her name. Perhaps she didn't have one because she had lost who she was in all of her "husbands".

So I felt like basically, and this may be a bit much, but Jesus described her to be what we call today; a THOT. Yes, a Thirsty Hoe Over There. This woman was thirsty and she was a hoe. There was obviously a thirst she was trying to quench that was insatiable because she was on her sixth "husband"! Her desire was clearly for man! The reason why the woman could not go to the well when the other women went is because she was ashamed and they must have been talking about her saying, "Look at that Thirsty Hoe Over There!" They knew about her six "husbands"!

Perhaps the Samaritan Woman's desire for these men was a symptom of what she had gone through in life just like me. The scripture doesn't go that deep but as a woman I feel like we have a connection and I know her life because she is me.

We have all had a THOT moment. We have all been the Samaritan Woman but I don't care how many "husbands" or men we have bedded in our quest for tangible companionship, comfort, and security, Jesus showed in His choice of route, fatigue, hunger, thirst, and rule breaking that He will go out of His way to see about us and meet us where we are; even in our THOTness. Jesus said that He has Living Water that He wants to fill us with so that we never thirst again, so that we never feel empty again, and we don't make the mistake of "doing us" or making those "make me feel good" phone calls. Be filled and stay full.

A Sip of Wisdom

I rededicated my life back to Jesus in this moment. Now this did not mean that I was perfect but it meant that I was going to make a conscientious effort to give Him control of my life. I decided that I was going to engage in a TRUE RELATIONSHIP with Him. Relationships have ups and downs but know that Jesus will never leave you or forsake you. We learned through the Samaritan Woman's story that He will meet you where you are and go out of His way to do so. If you are ready to give Him control of your life, engage in a true relationship with Him, and be saved, read John 3:16 and Romans 10:9. Then, read this prayer:

Hey Jesus,

Thank you for meeting me where I am right now in this moment. Thank you for loving me in spite of myself. I know that I am a sinner and I have some things to work on within myself. I ask for your forgiveness. I believe you died on the cross for my sins and rose from the dead with all power. Please show me that same power lives in me to conquer myself and my mess. Teach me how to trust you as Lord and Savior over my life. As I pursue you, show me how you see me and teach me to love myself. Give me a desire for you and your Word so that I can hear you clearly, fall in love with you, and make you smile with my actions. In Your Name I Pray, Amen.

Random THOT (Just Kidding) Thought: If you are wondering once again, how I got all of that from reading the passage of scripture, I literally asked God to show me what He wanted me to see before I started reading that day. The scripture about the Samaritan Woman's five husbands really intrigued me. Then I used my favorite search engine on the internet to search commentaries. I always try to relate the bible to what I go through daily and as you can see, even though they were in a different time period, the life issue and message is still relevant today.

Ask God to give you a desire for His Word. That is the best way to start hearing His voice. When you go to pray, just talk to Him; tell God exactly how you feel. Sometimes I write it down or just speak aloud. Either way you do it, He wants to hear from you today.

Chapter 13

Dear Samaritan Woman

What did you do with the husband Jesus told you about?

This, I had to know. After the Samaritan Woman had her encounter with Jesus, what did she do with the man that Jesus told her to go get? What do you do when you have decided to give your life to Jesus, fully walk in your purpose, and you have a man in whom you cannot let go? The scripture never really says what she did with him and I needed to know because Big Daddy was back.

Man, for the life of me, I am trying to remember how I let him back in and I honestly don't—yes I do! As I recollect, I am reminded of how crafty the devil is. he got me.

It was a sunny afternoon and my children were taking a nap; they had to have been because they were quiet. I was cleaning my kitchen of the remnants from lunch. It was the Saturday before Resurrection Sunday; the last full day of my fast to stay focused. My Struggle and I weren't talking much anymore. In fact, we weren't talking at all.

My phone rang randomly and as I looked at the screen, I tilted my head in consideration of answering. He was no longer a contact in my phone but I recognized the phone number. Hello?

Surprisingly, after all we'd been through, we had the most productive conversation that day. We conversed briefly about the past and our current relationship statuses. He was going through something. What? I do not remember but I actually got to minister words of encouragement. The conversation was the epitome of closure. It ended with him asking if we were cool and if he could call sometime; I said yes. Initially, it was easy going. I didn't hear from him every day and that was just fine with me because I really didn't want him back in my life. I kept my distance for quite some time because I was fighting hard to stay focused but somehow, we got back into the flow of things.

We started conversing every day. Let's just call it what it was: We were "talking." I hate that term. I was falling back into the flow of a relationship without a title. He was coming around more and I even met him for ice cream once, "just to talk."

I started to like where our relationship was going. He seemed different than before. I was staying focused and I felt like we were in the beginning stages of me learning to trust him again. I told him I needed to trust him if we were going to be cool and eventually be friends. The attraction had always been there but sex was out of the question because I made sure to reiterate that I was celibate. For the first time in my life I was setting standards and sticking to my morals and values, which felt really good. But it got to the point where I had to reiterate it to myself because the attraction has always been heavy between me and Big Daddy.

One night, he asked me to come over. I had a sitter because I was already out. I wanted to go. When I initially went out, I had already planned in the back of my mind to go to his house after. As I left the event to head to his house, I got convicted. "Go home," I heard. I felt an uneasiness in my stomach but I wanted to see him so bad. I missed his face. All this talking on the phone was getting old but the conviction was strong. Right when I picked up my phone to tell him I was going home, I received a text from him: "I need you." He wanted me to help him with something that he probably could have done by himself but those words meant the world to me.

He said he needed me.
I'm still trying to decipher how and why the notion of a grown ass
man needing me—
Has the power to turn me on and off simultaneously.
He. Said. He. Needed. Me.
The combo of words that have the power to crumble my entire
resolve.
How I love to feel needed.
Codependency.
I helped him with the minute task and He.
Still.
Needed me.
He leaned in to hug me and in one fluid motion,
My bra was undone, left breast in mouth, & teeth on my neck.
Felt his need probe my thigh.
I mean it felt amazing but,
I needed more than to be groped, bit, and licked.
I needed him to realize that I am more than the rotund of my behind,
the juncture between my legs.
I needed more than meaningless words in the heat of passion.
He said he loved me.
But not enough to take my words seriously and respect my hurt and
healing.
As I pushed him away,
I realized that I finally love me more.

I love me more than your bull shit need.
I love me more than your opinion of me.
I love me more than giving you pleasure with the hope that you'll
remain interested.
I finally know who I am.
I know what I want.
I know what I need.
And I love me more than your need...

When will you love you more?

I remember leaving his house and simultaneously feeling victorious and guilty. I felt victorious because I didn't give in. I felt guilty because I put myself in the situation even though God told me to go home. When was I going to love and trust Him enough to adhere to what He was saying? I felt like I had just cheated on my man or something. The conviction was so real. In my mind I had let God down. I repented on the long, silent drive home, got home, kissed my kids goodnight, and slept a fitful sleep.

When I woke up the next morning to drive to work, I still felt ashamed. Normally on my drives to work I drive in silence, openly talk to God, or listen to my favorite morning show. This particular morning I simply road in silence; I had nothing to say to God. It kind of felt like that awkward drive home when your parent picks you up from doing something you had no business doing. I couldn't take the tension anymore so I simply said, "Lord, I'm so sorry" and began to cry silent tears. I heard Him say:

Just come to me.
I've always met you where you were.
Each time you surrendered all, I was right there with open arms.
I'm always here.
I have never left you.
I have never forsaken you.
You're the one who keeps leaving in shame.

YOU DONT HAVE TO BE PERFECT OR HAVE IT ALL TOGETHER
TO COME TO ME.
Just talk to me about it instead of hiding.
I see and know everything therefore you really aren't hiding;
I just see you covered by whatever is keeping you from me.
Come to me with it.
Don't hide.
I love you and we will work through it together.
Stop leaving in shame.

God is so faithful. His words made me fall more in love with Him and I began to keep my distance from Big Daddy because that was the only way I was going to stay focused.

I was doing so very well until my children went to spend the summer with their father. I was excited because I was getting a break but I missed them immensely. I got back home and I was so lonely. I was bored. There was only so much cooking and gardening I could do to keep myself occupied. I really didn't want to go out much because that's really not my forte. Big Daddy was right there to fill the void.

I started going back to his house once again. He was working on a personal project and I was working on mine; this book. He was pursuing his dream which was admirable and so was I. One day we planned for me to come over. I brought dinner and we said we would work individually and be productive but I could not work in his house. I didn't feel comfortable. He was working diligently but I could not get in my groove. Normally when I write, I pray and I have soft jazz playing. I had to invite God where I was to work and I know He was not pleased with where I was even if I was not doing anything. I was wasting time. I just could not work. I could not even brainstorm or form one productive thought. This really messed with me. Why couldn't I work around him?

You're thirsty (bored) when you are with him
Because he doesn't quench your thirst.

He doesn't provide nourishment and strength training
for what you are so desperately trying to fulfill.
Keep pouring without being poured into and you will end up empty.
In this season, you must only pour into people who pour into you.
Your life and purpose depend on it.

I stated that I was bored and lonely because my children were gone but I was still bored and lonely sitting up in his house with him. Like Jill Scott wrote, "I'm lonely whenever you're around."

Being around him just made my hormones rage. That was it. Now I talked a lot about pouring and staying full but this man was still sexy whether he had the capacity to quench my thirst or not. I could not take that away from him.

It was 40% I wanna do this
And 60% I might as well.
I mean my shirt was off.
Felt cool air on my nipples after I TOLD HIM to go get a condom in a
"Fuck it" tone.
He came back and told me to ride it.
I couldn't initiate my sin so I told him to do it.
He put it in and I wanted it.
This want has been crazy.
This need has been torture.
I snapped and pushed him away.
Grabbed my clothes and left without looking back.
While I laid there, my mind raced:
I can't let God down. Too many people depend on me.
This is not about me.
This doesn't even feel how I thought it would feel.
I can't let God down.
I can't keep doing this.

I felt like crap. I had made the same mistake again. I rationalized with myself about whether or not I had sex. I felt myself slipping in guilt and shame. I didn't want to do anything; write, cook, clean, eat; nothing. I was basically stressing myself out. The struggle was real. I could feel the tug of war going on inside of me with Big Daddy on one side and God on the other. I had to do something.

One day I met him to talk about what happened at his house. It was my plan to explain to him why I couldn't sleep with him. In our conversation, he mentioned that lately when we spoke, I had this stank look on my face like I didn't like him or something. We eventually got into an argument about what I was doing in pursuing my purpose and I ranted back that it is my mission to help women become whole and healthy individuals who lean solely on God and walk in their purpose rather than chasing men and a happily ever after. I remember saying that it was my desire that women realize that they are the prize and never settle for anyone less than the man God has for them.

In that moment, I realized I was doing just that; settling. In my rant, I reminded myself of my mission and got my focus back. I wanted him to understand so badly but he didn't. It wasn't his fault; it wasn't his vision to understand. It was time to let go.

My cousin randomly texted me the following Sunday the notes from a message her pastor preached. One particular question stood out to me:

How many people truly understand where you are going in life right now?

A Sip of Wisdom

It was time to let go. From my journal: *"Here I am back where I started. I didn't give him my body but I opened up my heart. I guess. I didn't even realize I was doing it. I feel empty. I've lost focus. But I felt like I was focused."*

I had fallen back into our way of doing things; talking multiple times throughout the day but I was still not giving it up. I refused to sleep with him. I was stuck in a writer's block. I was beginning to be stressed out because I felt like I was disappointing God because I was idle. I wanted to finish my assignment but I was holding on to this relationship. He wanted sex. I promise I wanted to give him what he needed but I could not compromise my call. I also felt like we had bigger issues than my celibacy.

"If you think a man is going to be with you, accept your kids, and you not giving him no sex…"

I felt very low with that statement but it helped me cut the relationship off. I went to God and began to think about where He brought me from: pure hell, depression, anxiety attacks, stress, and I could not go back there. He has plans for me and I could not delay or deter them any longer.

Dear Samaritan Woman,

Did you feel the way I do now; empty and alone?
I know Jesus is here.
I feel Him but did you feel like this
while preaching the gospel around the world?
Even after your encounter with Christ,
did you have this one guy in whom you could not let go?
Was he handsome and caring?
Did he not complement you as you grew in your walk with Christ?
Was he, in fact, almost your complete opposite
and you still wanted him to be there?
Did the fact that you knew it wouldn't work
make you question and be discouraged about your whole purpose
and conscious of the fact that you were doing this more for Christ
and His people than yourself?
Love,
Thirsty

I wrote that piece while sobbing in my bed after getting off of the phone from cutting it off with Big Daddy. The pulling in my gut to let him go was so great and I was fighting against it so hard.

It was time to fast. Fasting is the only way I regain my focus. I wanted this man out of my mind and I wanted to finish my assignment; this book. So I decided to fast from social networks and anything that did not promote me finishing my assignment. In my opinion, fasting is like rehab. There will be symptoms of withdrawal.

I let him in. Again. Not all the way in.
But just enough for me to be typing this with tears streaming down
my face.
Headphones in my ears. Fred Hammond playing. At my desk at
work.

Fasting. To get him out.
I woke up this morning.
He was the first thing on my mind.
I began asking God questions:
Is he with her? Why does it matter?
After all the hurt and pain and letting go,
getting close to Christ,
being free,
learning my purpose,
walking in my purpose;
and I still let him in.
Thinking we could be friends.
But friendship doesn't feel like that.
I have friends. Good ones.
And they don't do or say things that compel me to feel low.
Why did I let him back in?
Maybe I was lonely.
I don't know.
Can I just be real?
After being strong for everyone else.
After being used to give someone else a Word,
I wanted someone big and strong to hold me and be my strength.
I wanted someone.
Not just someone.
My man even though he was not OFFICIALLY my man,
to impart a Word to me.
To just BE THERE DAMMIT.
He didn't understand me being strong for everyone else.
He didn't understand Christ using me.
Maybe I didn't either because
I Still Let Him In.

At the end of the day, I have moments where I feel like this; like I want someone big and strong to be my strength. I have learned to lean on God in these moments. He has shown himself to be the perfect comforter. I have gone so far as to make a contact in my phone when I feel like texting. There are times that I simply do not feel like praying or talking to God. In those moments, to avoid texting someone else to make me feel good, I text Jesus. (777-777-7777). Don't judge me. Try it.

I'm gonna need more than a devotion to get through this one.
Although, my morning devotion did confirm some things this morning.
More than gospel music playing nonstop in my ears.
I decided that I need to really get my life after lurking on his social network pages.
Confession: I lurked on hers too.
I will not get back to the point where I am comparing myself to anyone.
I will not get back to the point where I am I looking for clues to validate my feelings or decisions.
I will not start regretting where I am today.
I am where I am supposed to be.
Learning and growing.
I will learn and grow from this.

You decide when you are going to be free. Remember, a stronghold is not a stronghold because it has a hold on you but because you have a strong hold on it. Let it go. I am a master lurker. If you want details on your baby daddy's girlfriend's auntie, I probably can find them. I cheated my fast and ended up even more miserable but the revelation was great.

You were not good for me. I let you go.
You started being good to her.
Now I want you back? To keep you from her?
Ok look. Fuck that.
I'm tired of my mood being swayed with every breath you take.
Every move you make.
Yes I know your moves. And her's too.
Time for me to wholeheartedly focus on my moves separate from you.
She wins.
I am a two handed string puppet. Limp and idle.
Allowing myself to be manipulated by your left hand and her right.
I'm cutting the strings.

She wins.
My head is held high only when you lift it.
My head bows low only when you lift hers.
Where is my backbone?
She wins.
I am older. She is younger.
She wins.
I am beautiful. She is pretty.
Ok. She's beautiful.
She wins.
I am careful. She is carefree. Just like you.
She wins.
I am wise. I am intelligent. I am worth it.
I don't know her. I DON'T NEED TO.
She wins.
I don't want you but I want you because she has you.
She has you.
You.
The one I let go because you were not good for me.
You.
Be good to her.
She wins.
I have me.
Me.
Be good to me.
I win.

A Sip of Wisdom

I was finally free. As I stated earlier, I am not sure whether God places people in your life so that you can learn certain lessons or if the enemy places people in your life and God decides He's going to the glory from the situation if you fall prey to the distraction. Either way, from this situation with Big Daddy, I finally set some standards for myself. I also stopped comparing myself to other women. I realized that I really didn't want him in my life. I just didn't want him to be with anyone else. He wasn't mine to begin with so why did it matter? He wasn't supposed to be my focus anyway so why was this even relevant? I learned to stop chasing things that weren't mine. I was reminded that I am the prize and I deserve to be pursued; not for my body but for who God MADE me to be.

I went to bible study the Wednesday right before my deadline for this book; my assignment and dream. I've always wanted to write a book. On the way there, I heard God say: "You will get your breakthrough tonight."

Praise and worship was amazing. Bishop gave the announcements and said, "Turn to John chapter 4." I immediately gasped! Wow! He was about to teach on The Samaritan Woman. All I could do was smile. I started this journey of writing this book officially around the time of Resurrection Sunday. God told me to study the book of John and I couldn't get past this woman's story. Resurrection Sunday was at the end of April and here it was the end of July. Right when I was feeling defeated because of my own actions and feeling like this journey was in vain, God used my Bishop to teach on this woman and the revelation God gave him amazed and ultimately freed me.

Hey Thirsty,

never went back. I never thirsted again. When I met Jesus, I was tired and thirsty in my spirit just like He was, naturally, when He met me. I was fatigued in my spirit just like He was, naturally, when He met me. I was alone even though I had someone waiting at home. The someone I had waiting at home never really knew me. None of them took the time to know me. Then again, I never really knew how to get a man to want to get to know me. They only liked what I had to offer, what I could do with my mouth, and what I could accomplish with my body. Then again, that was the only way I knew how to get their attention. It was a win/win situation because I quenched their thirst and they quenched mine; my thirst of wanting someone there even if they weren't really there for me. Everyone knew about them. Everyone knew what I was doing but they did not understand why. I knew they talked about me. I made a name for myself. No one knew what I was going through.

That day at the well, I was so tired. I dragged myself there to draw water but that day changed my very life. I met Jesus. He was the first man to not say anything to me about my body when He met me. In fact, He asked me for water. Yep. Asked me for water and said nothing about this 32-29-40. Wow. That was all I ever wanted; for someone to finally see me for me even if I didn't know who that was. I was searching for that all along and here He was finally; My Messiah. My Savior. Now that I think about it, He asked me for water and took the time to talk to me even though He ALREADY KNEW me. He already knew what everyone else knew and HE STILL offered me this Living Water that "became a fresh, bubbling spring within me, giving me eternal life." And I never thirsted again.

Listen Thirsty, He's been right there all along offering you this Living Water. Aren't you tired? Aren't you over drinking and still being thirsty? This whole book has been about you knowing your worth and someone finally seeing you for you and all you have inside of you. Well here He is. Drink and never thirst again.

Love,

The Samaritan Woman

P. S. Make sure you tell your story to everyone that was talking about you anyway. Jesus wants to quench their thirst as well.

Conclusion

Anytime I have made the decision to pursue me, my process always starts with a distraction. We experience the most distractions when we make the decision to pursue who we are, cultivate our gifts, and walk in our purpose. Be conscientious that in learning your purpose, you have to realize that you are not here for yourself. We are here to impact others and lead people to Christ. I now realize that if I am not freed from putting a man before God then other people may not be free.

Cutting my distraction off is normally followed by me surrendering to God. I had to learn that I am not perfect. Discipleship is a process in which one strives to be more like Christ. This does not mean that we should continuously sin to repent but it means learning who Christ is, falling in love, and making our actions say such.

There is deliverance through transparency. I believe that we are not effective as a church because we are afraid to look anything other than perfect. We cannot forget where we come from and how God brought us out. The change we want to see in ourselves or the change that we have seen in ourselves is the change we are suppose to make in the world.

God has led me to share my testimony in great detail with people similar to how the Samaritan Woman did to compel people to follow Jesus. God is something else. He has brought me through a great deal and variety of situations. He has equipped me with the gift of writing for release and freedom for myself and others.

Your gifts are where your freedom lies. Do not allow the enemy to shut up your gift.

In surrendering to God, He is freeing me from my stronghold. You guessed it right. Men have been flocking to me like flies at a cookout; old boos and new janks. However, through this, God is teaching me my worth. He is showing me how to set standards as a Woman of Him. He is revealing to me how to completely lean on Him. He is healing me completely. Initially, I thought to myself, as you read earlier, that the Samaritan woman went back home to her sixth husband however, she did not. I now realize that she was tired and when you get tired to the point where you simply cannot get it wrong, you will seek and stick with getting it right.

As God is freeing me from my stronghold, He is using me to free every person with the same stronghold in my circle of influence. I realize that I had to go through my process because someone else will need to relate and get free.

The process is not a bad thing. It sounds like a hazing or something right? It is where we truly learn the depth of God's love. It is where we learn the difference between God and the enemy's voice. It is where people will fall off who are not supposed to be in our lives. It is where God will introduce us to new people. It is where we gain discipline and wisdom. It is where the enemy's tactics are exposed. It is where we learn and value how God sees us. It is where we learn and grasp our worth. It is where we find contentment in His presence.

The process is the epitome of:

"And we know that God causes everything to work together for the good of those who love God and are called according to his purpose for them."
Romans 8:28

Now all you have to do is stay focused. Distractions and disappointments will come but remember, as my Bishop says, they are just that: things and people to diss your traction and appointment to where God has called you to be.

Remember that Jesus loves you just the way you are. There is nothing you have done that will make him not love you or love you any less.

Can anything ever separate us from Christ's love? Does it mean he no longer loves us if we have trouble or calamity, or are persecuted, or hungry, or destitute, or in danger, or threatened with death? (As the Scriptures say, "For your sake we are killed every day; we are being slaughtered like sheep." No, despite all these things, overwhelming victory is ours through Christ, who loved us. And I am convinced that nothing can ever separate us from God's love. Neither death nor life, neither angels nor demons, neither our fears for today nor our worries about tomorrow—not even the powers of hell can separate us from God's love. No power in the sky above or in the earth below—indeed, nothing in all creation will ever be able to separate us from the love of God that is revealed in Christ Jesus our Lord.
Romans 8:35-39

He knows you and what you are going to do before you do it. The emptiness you have, He will fill it. The thirst you have, He will quench. Stay FOCUSED!

How do you pour and stay full?

1. By drinking the Living Water Jesus has for you and staying focused.
2. By only pouring into entities that pour into you.

#21DaysOfMe©

O K! So by now you are probably like, "Where do I go from here?" The first thing I suggest is that you recondition yourself to focus on you, God, and His plan for your life.

As women, we have the most challenging time just focusing on us. While we are single, we are planning our weddings. While we are married, we put ourselves last to promote the wellbeing of our families. And as mothers, we will die and kill ourselves for our children. It's time to live. If you are not healthy, what you govern will be sick as well. No more "getting back to me" when things crumble. During these 21 Days, I pray that you "Reclaim Me!"

#21DaysOfMe© was a social media campaign my team conducted that proved to be very effective in the emotional well-being of women. I challenge you to complete it for the next 21 days.

For the next 21 Days, I challenge you to focus on you. I don't care where you are in life; single, married, and/or a mother; you need to take this time for yourself!

There are 5 rules to this:

1. Get a journal to release your thoughts and actions.
2. Do the first thing that comes to mind when you read the specific challenge for each day. DON'T OVER THINK IT.
3. Do not involve ANYONE ELSE in your Me Day Activity, it's all about you.
4. Do not spend a whole bunch of money.

5. Some Days will CHALLENGE you. Just remember these days are about healing and transparency leads to deliverance.

Day1. Save ME
Day2. Pamper ME
Day3. Love ME
Day4. Future ME
Day5. Rescue ME
Day6. Amaze ME
Day7. Forgive ME
Day8. Entertain ME
Day9. Know ME
Day10. Detox ME
Day11. Proud of ME
Day12. Date ME
Day13. Father ME
Day14. Celebrate ME
Day15. Define ME
Day16. Explore ME
Day17. Wine ME
Day18. Free ME
Day19. All about ME
Day20. Flawless ME
Day21. Pursue ME

Made in the USA
Middletown, DE
22 December 2021